D1609680

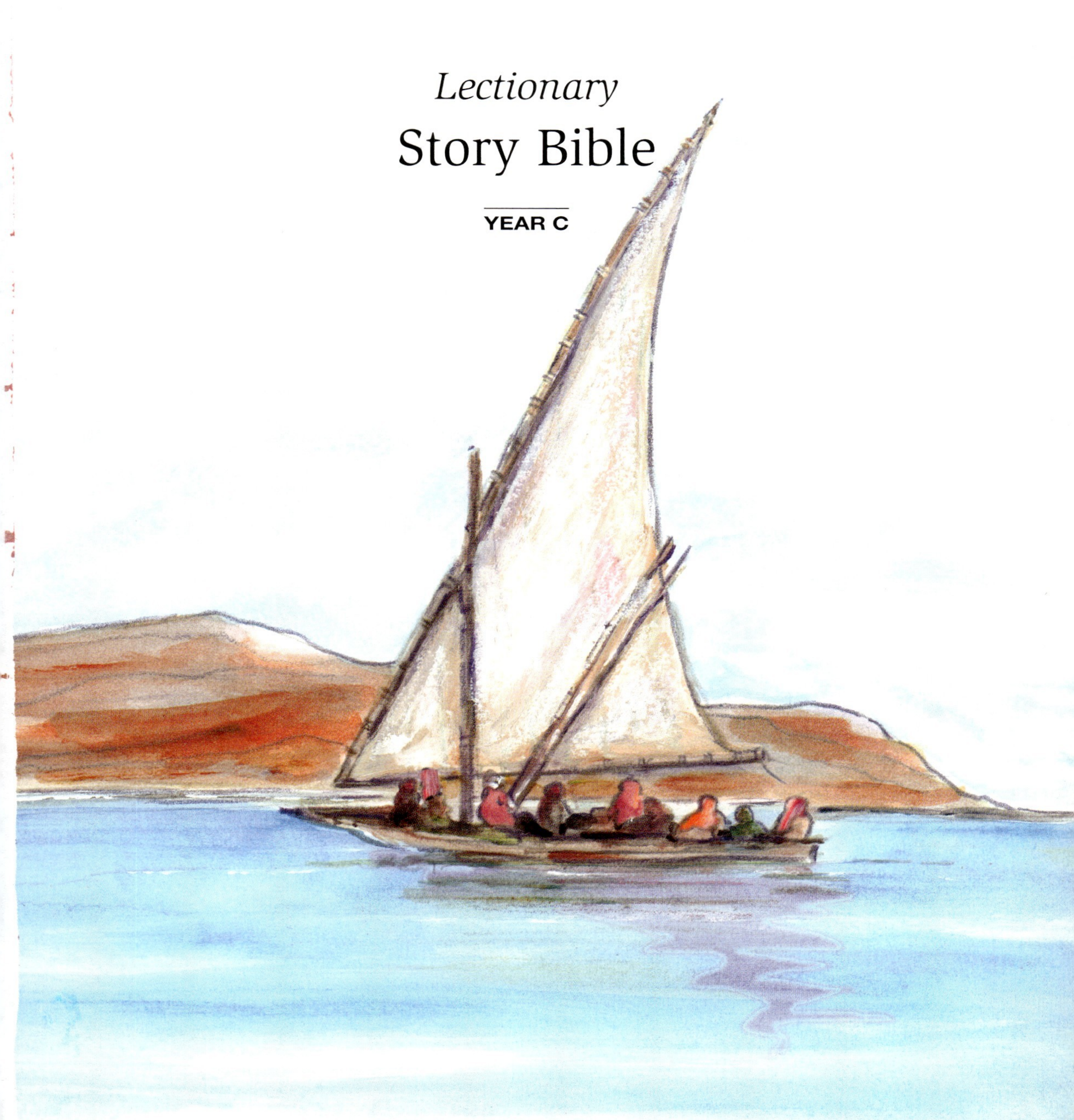

Lectionary

Story Bible

YEAR C

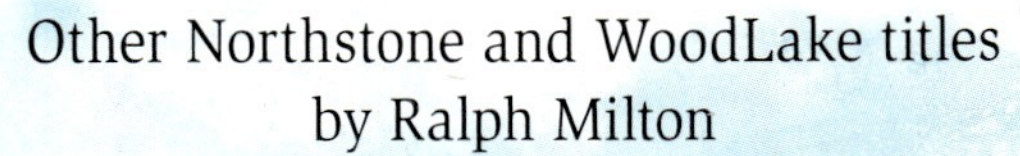
Other Northstone and WoodLake titles
by Ralph Milton

Sermon Seasonings
God for Beginners
Is This Your Idea of a Good Time, God?
Man to Man
This United Church of Ours
The Family Story Bible
Angels in Red Suspenders
Julian's Cell
The Essence of Julian
The Spirituality of Grandparenting
Lectionary Story Bible Year A and B
Lectionary Story Bible Year Set

Ralph Milton

Lectionary
Story Bible

YEAR C

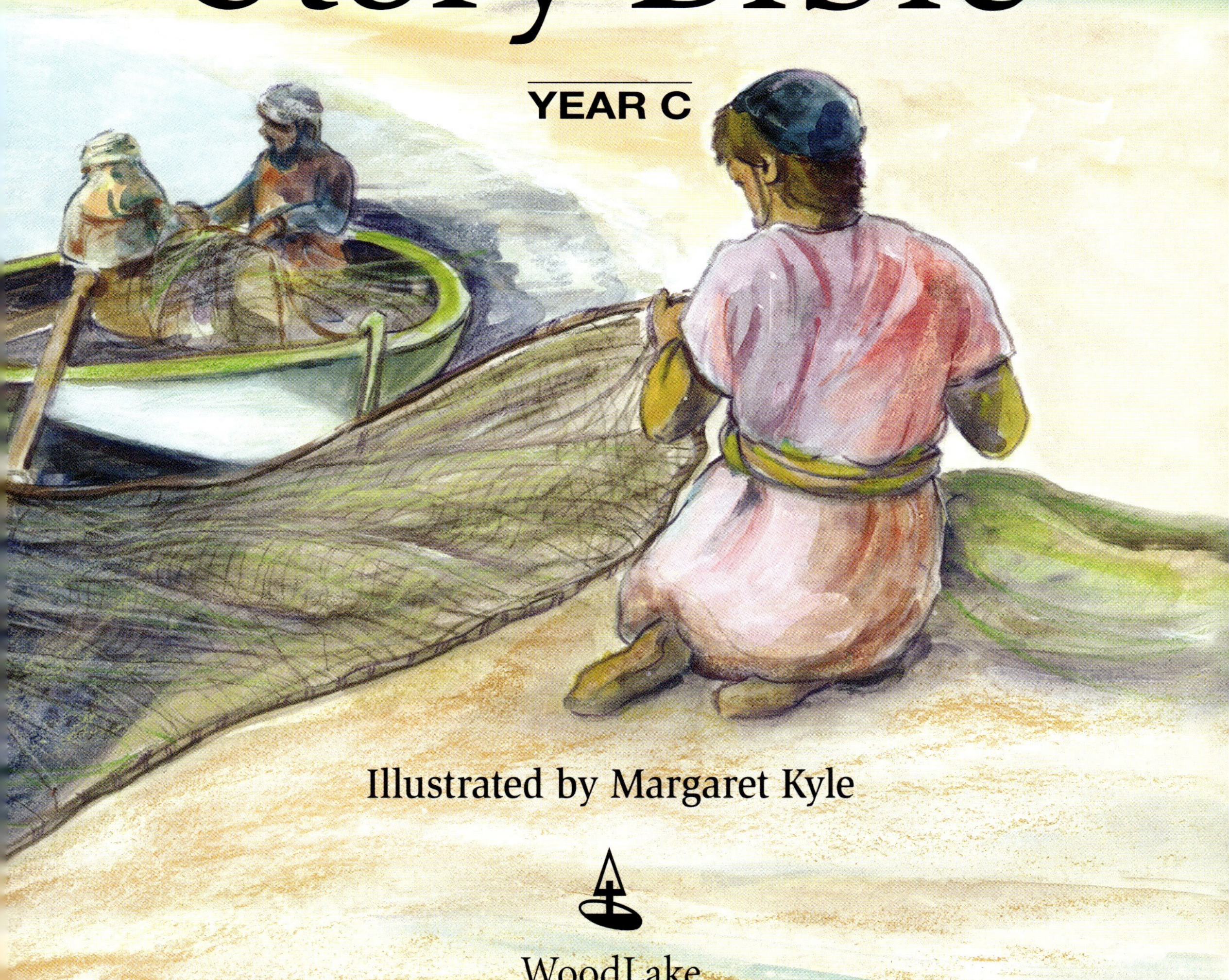

Illustrated by Margaret Kyle

WoodLake

Editors: Cathie Talbot and Michael Schwartzentruber
Interior design: Verena Velten
Cover design: Margaret Kyle
Proofreader: Dianne Greenslade

At Wood Lake Publishing, we practise what we publish, being guided by a concern for fairness, justice, and equal opportunity in all of our relationships with employees and customers. Wood Lake Publishing is an employee-owned company, committed to caring for the environment and all creation. Wood Lake Publishing recycles, reuses, and encourages readers to do the same. Resources are printed on 100% post-consumer recycled paper and more environmentally friendly groundwood papers (newsprint), whenever possible. A percentage of all profit is donated to charitable organizations.

Library and Archives Canada Cataloguing in Publication
Milton, Ralph
Lectionary story Bible / Ralph Milton ; illustrated by Margaret Kyle.
Includes bibliographical references and index.
Contents: Vol. 1. Year A - v. 2. Year B - v. 3. Year C.
ISBN 978-1-55145-547-1 (Year A). – ISBN 978-1-55145-564-8 (Year B). –
ISBN 978-1-55145-576-1 (Year C)
1. Bible stories, English. I. Kyle, Margaret
II. Title. III. Title: Story Bible.
BS551.3.M54 2007 j220.9'505 C2007-901279-5
BS551.3

Published by WoodLake
An imprint of Wood Lake Publishing Inc.
9590 Jim Bailey Road,
Kelowna, BC, Canada, V4V 1R2
www.woodlakebooks.com
250.766.2778

Printing 10 9 8 7 6 5 4 3 2 1
Printed in China

Contents

Have Fun!

A word to parents and leaders

The Bible is full of stories – from heroic sagas, to knee-slapping humour, to romance and mystery. It's the *stories* in the Bible that appeal to children most and that appeal to *me* most. I think that's the part of the Bible most adults delight in, too, even though they may not admit it.

The lectionary

This is the third and final volume in a series of three *Lectionary Story Bibles* based on scripture readings from the *Revised Common Lectionary* (RCL). These books are designed for those who would like to supplement a lectionary-based Christian education resource, such as *Seasons of the Spirit,* or for those who would like to read stories at home to supplement their church experience.

A lectionary provides an ordered system of reading the Bible, with two readings from the Hebrew scriptures (sometimes called the Old Testament) and two readings each week from the Christian scriptures (traditionally called the New Testament).

Different denominations use different versions of the lectionary. Some of the stories included in this book may not be included in the scripture readings listed in the version of the lectionary used by your church.

You may be familiar with *The Family Story Bible.* It's a collection of stories that are presented in the order in which they appear in the Bible. All of those stories are included in this series of three *Lectionary Story Bibles.* Here they are presented in the order in which they appear in the lectionary, along with new stories based on other scripture readings from the lectionary – about three times as many as in *The Family Story Bible.*

Be like a child

A lectionary is a very useful tool, but it was designed by folks who were more concerned about the teachings of the Bible than about the stories. In other words, it was designed for adults. Sometimes it skips over the tops of stories, or picks out a few short passages from a longer, exciting saga. That's why, in many cases, my stories are based on more of the text than is recommended by the lectionary.

I try to tell the story from beginning to end, even when the scripture passages suggested by the lectionary don't. That's also why you'll find stories in these three volumes that are in the Bible but not in the lectionary. I've tried to fill in the blanks.

The Bible is not a book of rules or a set of moral precepts that we somehow absorb and then order our lives by, although some contemporary churches encourage this view. Traditional Christianity says that when we're open to the "word of God," God will speak to us *through* the Bible. So I'm asking you to approach the Bible with a kind of childlike openness.

Jesus said it first: "Unless you become like a little child, you cannot enter God's realm" (Matthew 18:3).

Imagination and passion

I'm a storyteller, not a theologian or a Bible scholar. The two most important things I bring to the task of telling Bible stories for children are imagination and passion.

First, imagination.

Where the terse biblical text offers little detail, I add my own. Where names are missing, I invent them. Where connecting narrative is absent, I supply it. Then I add my own dash of drama and suspense and fun. Sometimes, almost the whole story comes from my imagination and almost none of it from the Bible, though I've tried very hard to preserve the *intention* of the scripture reading.

As a professional writer, my imagination is not tamed, but it *is* disciplined. I do my research. The details I imagine are checked to make sure they have textual, historical, and theological validity. I've taken many biblical courses, done graduate work in Israel, and read hundreds of books in order to be able to do this. But still, the imagination that weaves these stories out of the raw material of the Bible is wild and childlike, and some people will find that profoundly disturbing.

Second, passion.

I believe with a deep and profound passion that God wants us to be a joyful, just, and caring people. One of the ways (but by no means the *only* way) God chose to help us be that kind of people was to encourage a particular people (the Hebrews) at a particular time (the biblical era) to record the stories of their struggles and sorrows, their joys and hopes.

They collected all kinds of writings – legends, folklore, stories, poems, fiction, history, recipes, and laws, and a dash here and there of utter drivel – into a book which we call the Bible.

The Bible can be a source of insight and wisdom and fun for adults and children. If we're open, God can speak to us through the stories of the Bible.

And when God speaks, it's never boring.

So enjoy each story, whether you think it is historically true, pure fiction, or somewhere in between. The inner truth, the wisdom, lives *inside* the story. Don't look for some pious little moral, but be open to a flash of insight into what it means to be spiritual human beings who live in families and communities with other spiritual human beings.

Let God speak to the child in you.

Enjoy!

Thanks

It's always impossible to thank all those involved in a project like this. For instance, there are all the folks who have offered appreciation and helpful comments about *The Family Story Bible* and who have made it a bestseller.

Specific thanks go to Zoë, my granddaughter, who offered helpful comments about many of the stories; to my life partner, Bev, who, as always, is my first, best, and toughest critic; to Mike Schwartzentruber, editor of Wood Lake Publishing, for his editing; and to Cathie Talbot, editor of *Seasons of the Spirit,* who read all the stories and offered wise and helpful comments.

But the biggest word of thanks goes to Margaret Kyle for the inspired artwork she has provided. She has taken this book (as she did with *The Family Story Bible*) from being acceptable to being exceptional.

– R.M.

I want to thank *all* my colleagues at Wood Lake Publishing for their support, and its co-founder Ralph Milton, for the opportunity to illustrate these stories.

Ralph has a way of finding the loving and gentle heart in even the most difficult Bible stories, and then of connecting that to life in a way in which children and adults can relate. My aim was not to illustrate every aspect of the story, but to paint one or two images symbolizing this loving and gentle heart.

I would also like to thank my husband, Michael Schwartzentruber, for his honest feedback, as well as his patience. I value his wisdom and insight.

I would like to dedicate this volume to our grandchild, Hanna Margareta Vouladakis.

– M.K.

The pages in this book are colour-coded to match the seasons of the church year:

Advent – *blue*
Christmas/Epiphany – *gold/white*
The Season after Epiphany – *green*
Lent – *purple*
Holy Week – *red*
Easter – *gold/white*
Pentecost – *red*
The Season after Pentecost – *green*

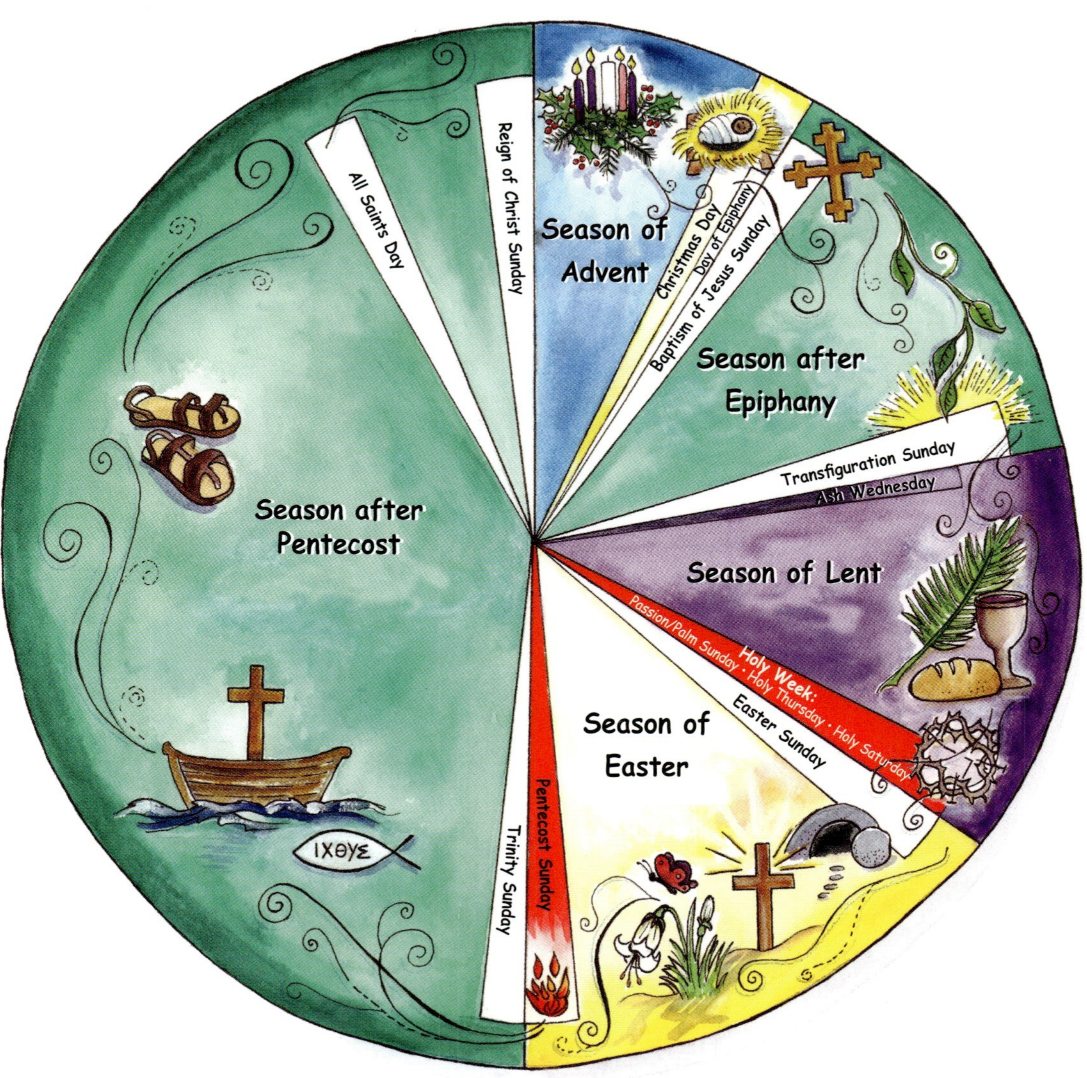

The Seasons of the Church Year and the Lectionary

The seasons of the church year form a unique rhythm by which Christians can live their lives. The rhythm follows the flow of the life of Jesus and is further enhanced by the melody of a lectionary, which establishes a sequence of scriptures over the liturgical seasons.

The year begins with **Advent**, four Sundays leading up to Christmas Day. These four weeks invite us to prepare ourselves spiritually for the birth of Jesus. Blue, representing hope, is often used as the symbolic colour of this season.

The season of **Christmas** begins the evening of December 24, and lasts for 12 days. This is a joyous season, celebrating the birth of Jesus through to the arrival of the magi at the feast of the **Epiphany** (January 6). White and gold suggest joy and glory.

The time from the Epiphany until the beginning of Lent is the **Season after the Epiphany** or Ordinary Time. The colour green, for growth and new life, serves as a backdrop for stories of the call of disciples and prophets, and of the beginnings of Jesus' ministry.

Lent consists of the 40 days before Easter. Because each Sunday is a little Easter, these days were not included in the counting. Lent is one of the oldest observances in the church's history. In ancient times when baptisms were held annually at Easter, candidates for baptism were required to spend some time in preparation. The 40 days of Lent compared to the 40 days that Jesus spent in the wilderness prior to his ministry. Over time, this period of fasting and reflection prior to Easter became popular for all Christians. The colour purple supports a mood of penitence.

Lent ends with Palm/Passion Sunday and Holy Week – a time to remember Jesus' arrest, trial, and crucifixtion. Palm/Passion Sunday, on the 6th week of Lent, is symbolized by the colour red.

After confronting the reality of crucifixion, Christians can exalt in the unbridled joy of resurrection at **Easter.** This great joyous season goes for 50 days celebrating that Christ is risen. The season reaches a wonderful conclusion with the feast of **Pentecost**, celebrating the presence of the Holy Spirit and the birth of the church. Traditionally, bright reds and oranges light up this day.

After the day of Pentecost we return to Ordinary Time – the **Season after Pentecost.** It generally covers about half the year, taking us back to Advent where the cycle begins again. In this lengthy season, we remember again the presence of God with us in the everyday.

The Mediterranean World of the New Testament

Black Sea
THRACE
Byzantium
BITHYNIA & PONTUS
GALATIA
N
W
E
S
MYSIA
Troas
Adramyttium
Pergamum
esbos
CAPPADOCIA
PHRYGIA
Antioch
Iconium
hios
Lydia
Commagene
Lycaonia
Lystra
Ephesus
Pisidia
Derbe
Samos
Tarsus
Antioch
CILICIA
Caria
PAMPHYLIA
Cnidus
Perga
Attalia
Cos
LYCIA
Myra
Patara
Rhodes
SYRIA
Salamis
Cyprus
Paphos
Phoenicia
Abilene
Sidon
Tyre
Damascus
Mediterranean Sea
Caesarea
Jerusalem
Dead Sea
Gaza
Judea
Alexandria
Memphis
EGYPT
Red Sea
= some of the places Paul visited during his travels to establish and encourage early church communities
0
75
150 miles
0
120.7
241.4 km

FIRST SUNDAY IN ADVENT

How to Be a Church Together

BASED ON 1 THESSALONIANS 3:9–13

Paul liked to tell people about his friend Jesus. He liked to tell them how much God loved them, and how to live God's way.

Paul and his two friends, Silvanus and Timothy, went to visit people who lived in a city with a very big name. Thessalonica. They stayed there for a long time telling people stories of Jesus and showing them how to live – how to be kind and gentle with each other.

Some of the people of Thessalonica said, "We could become a church. We could come together to pray and sing. We could do things together to help others. There are people in our city who don't have enough to eat and who don't have a place to live. We could help them."

Paul and his friends were very happy when the people decided to become a church. "Now you can help teach each other more about God, and about how to live in God's way," he said. "Now Silvanus and Timothy and I can go to other places to tell people about God's love."

Many days after they had left, Silvanus said to Paul, "I miss the people of Thessalonica. They were kind and gentle people. I think they will become a good, strong church together."

"That's what our friend Timothy said when he came and told us about the church in Thessalonica," said Paul. "I think I'll send them a letter to tell them that. And maybe in my letter I can say some things that will help them grow together."

Here is part of the letter that Paul wrote to the Thessalonians. You can find Paul's letter in the Bible.

Dear friends in the church at Thessalonica

Silvanus and Timothy and I often think of you. We think of the good times we had with you, when we shared the stories of Jesus. Together we learned about God's love We think God chose you specially to be the church in your city. God had a dream for you – a dream of how you could be the church together. Timothy told me how you help each other and how you tell the stories of Jesus that you remember. You help people who don't have enough food, or clothing or a place to live.

We say thank you to God every day when we think of you. And oh, how we'd like to come and visit you again.

But until we are able to do that, we hope God will be with you in your life together as a church – that God will help you say and do kind and good things. And we hope that God will help you to love each other more and more, just as the three of us love you so very much.

In our prayers each day, we ask God to help you be strong, because we know it isn't easy to live God's way. It is hard being a church together, when other people never think about God.

So remember you are God's people. Please keep on being God's church. Pray often to God, and you will know how to love each other, and how to help others grow and live in God's way.

Please pray for us as we tell others about Jesus. And please give a hug to all our many friends in Thessalonica.

With love,
Paul

What Do Prophets Do?

BASED ON LUKE 21:25–36

One day, when Jesus was telling people about God, some of them asked a hard question.

"Jesus," they said. "Many people are saying things that make us feel afraid."

"What are they saying to you?" Jesus asked.

"They say there are bad things happening. Many people are fighting in wars. They are killing each other."

"You will hear about many such things," said Jesus. "The people who are telling about them are called prophets."

"Can prophets tell what is going to happen in the future?"

"No," said Jesus. "But they can help us get ready. When you see the buds on the trees and the first tiny leaves poke out, you know that it's springtime. You know that summer is coming and you can get ready. That's what prophets do. They look at the things that are happening around them. They help us remember how God has helped us in so many ways. And they help us get ready for the things that are going to happen."

"So what should we do?"

"Try really hard to live in God's way. Remember the stories I told you. Talk to God in your payers. Tell God what you are afraid of – what you are worried about. Ask God what you can do about the bad things that are happening. Then God will help you be strong and will help you know how to live – even when things are feeling scary."

SECOND SUNDAY IN ADVENT

Get Ready for a New Friend

BASED ON PORTIONS OF LUKE 1 AND LUKE 3

Note to leaders and parents: *The lectionary readings for this Sunday are Luke 1:68–79, which is Zechariah's song, and Luke 3:1–6, which is John's declaration about Jesus. We have chosen to combine the two stories and use other selected verses to tell a bit of the story of John the Baptizer.*

Suppose someone tells you, "You are going to have a new friend. That friend is coming to your house to play with you." What would you do to prepare for them?

Maybe you would ask some questions. "What is my new friend's name? What kinds of games does my new friend like to play?"

The Bible tells a story about a man named John, who came to tell people that God's Chosen One was coming. John came to tell the people to get ready.

The Bible also tells us a strange story about what happened when John was born. His mother, Elizabeth, and his father, Zechariah, were already very old. They thought they would ever never have a child.

One day, Zechariah was in the Temple praying to God. An angel came to him.

"God will give you and Elizabeth a baby," said the angel. "You will call him John, and he will help many people learn to love God."

Zechariah shook his head.

"You don't believe me?" said the angel to Zechariah. "Then you won't be able to talk until the baby is born."

When Zechariah came out of the Temple, he couldn't say a word. He had to write when he wanted to tell people something.

After a while, Elizabeth's baby was born. He was a strong, healthy boy. She and Zechariah took the new baby to their church, which was called a synagogue. They wanted to say "thank you" to God, and to give the baby a name. Zechariah still couldn't talk.

Everybody thought they would name the new baby after his father, Zechariah. In those days, the first baby boy was almost always named after his father.

"No," said Elizabeth. "The baby's name is John."

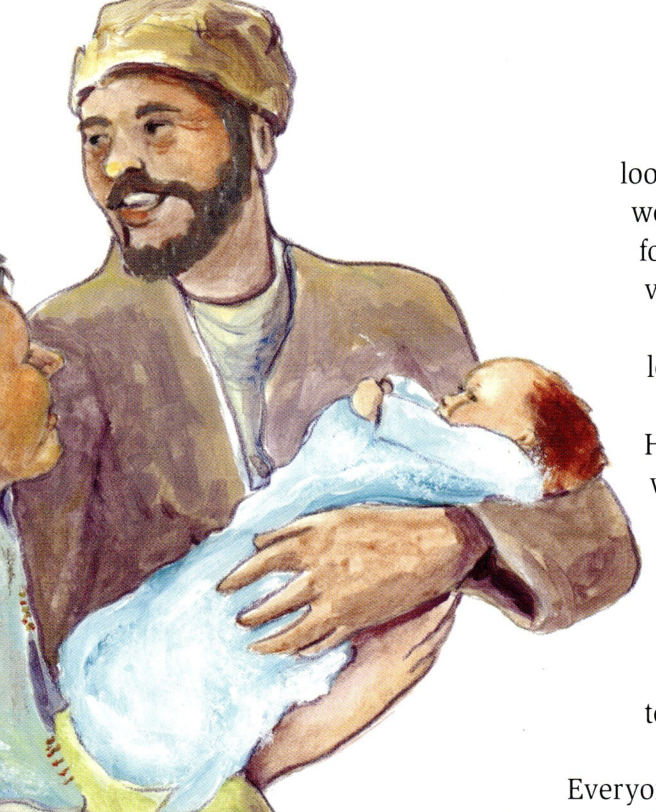

All the people in the synagogue looked at Zechariah. They thought he would be upset. Just then, Zechariah found he could talk again. In a loud voice, he said, “His name is John!”

And Zechariah began to sing in a loud, clear voice:

How wonderful is God
who comes to help us all.
God promised us a Chosen One,
a person kind and good.
And you, my little baby John,
you will get us ready.
You will help us all prepare,
to meet God’s Chosen One.

Everyone was surprised. They wondered about the strange things that had happened to Elizabeth and Zechariah. They wondered what kind of person little baby John would grow up to be.

When John grew up, he knew God had a special job for him. John prayed to God often, and in his prayers he heard God telling him to be a “messenger.”

“I have a message for you from God,” John told the people. “Come to the river Jordan with me. Let me dip you under the water, to wash you clean, so that you are ready for God’s Chosen One.”

John remembered the words to an old, old song. He learned the song from reading a book written by Old Isaiah. It was a song about getting ready.

Get yourself ready! Get yourself ready!
God is sending us a new friend,
and God wants us to be ready.
Tidy your room. Put on clean clothes.
Get ready! Get ready
for God’s Chosen One.

John didn’t know who God’s Chosen One would be. But as soon as he saw Jesus walking toward him, he knew. “This is the one we were expecting!” he shouted. “This is God’s Chosen One.”

Sing! Shout! Rejoice!

BASED ON ZEPHANIAH 3:14–20 AND PHILIPPIANS 4:4–7

Zephaniah was a prophet. He wrote a very short little book you can find in the Bible.

In his book, Zephaniah scolds the people of Israel. "You have not been living in God's way. You can do better than that!"

But Zephaniah also had happy things to say to the people of Israel. His happy words almost sound like a song.

All the girls should sing out loud!
All the boys should shout!
God is living right among you,
and God will make you glad.
So please don't be afraid again.
Smile and laugh and sing.
Those who can't walk will learn to run.
Lonely ones will find friends.
Then all the boys will sing out loud!
And all the girls will shout!

Many years after the prophet Zephaniah lived, a man named Paul wrote letters to his friends. One of his letters was to the church in Philippi. Part of this letter was also like a song.

Rejoice in your God always; again I say, Rejoice.
Rejoice in your God always; again I say, Rejoice.
Be gentle and kind to everyone.
Be gentle and kind to all.
Talk to God because God is your friend
and you will find peace in your heart.

Are You God's Chosen One?

BASED ON LUKE 3:7–18

Before Jesus began to tell people about God, his friend John was doing that. Some people called him John the Baptizer. That's because John would take people to the Jordan River. There he would hold them under the water for just a moment while he said a prayer to God.

That's called "baptism."

Sometimes John sounded a little bit angry. Even cranky. Sometimes he yelled at the people who came to be baptized.

"Who told you to come here to the Jordan River? If you are doing bad things – if you are not living God's way – then God already knows about it."

The people felt afraid. "What should we do?"

"Learn to share!" said John. "If you have two coats, share with the person who doesn't have even one. If you have food, don't keep it all to yourself. Share it with someone who is hungry."

A soldier came up to John. "What should I do?" he asked.

"Don't make people give you money just because you are a soldier and you have a sharp sword that can hurt people. Be kind to people instead."

John went to the Jordan River every day. Every day, he told people about God's love, and about God's Chosen One who would come.

Some of the people in the crowd wondered if John was the Messiah. "Are you the Chosen One?" they asked.

"No!" said John. "I am not God's Chosen One. I've been baptizing you in the water of the Jordan River. But God's Chosen One – God's Messiah – will baptize you with the Spirit. When that happens, it will almost feel like fire is burning inside of you. But the fire won't hurt you. You will feel clean and good and strong inside."

When someone said, "I really want to be a different kind of person. I really want to live God's way," John would smile.

"Come," he said. "Let me baptize you. Let me hold you under the water for just a moment while I say a little prayer to God. The water will make you clean on the outside, but God's love will make you clean on the inside."

FOURTH SUNDAY IN ADVENT

Mary, Elizabeth, and Their Babies

BASED ON LUKE 1:39–55

Note to leaders and parents: *The reference to Hannah (the mother of the prophet Samuel) can be found in 1 Samuel 2:1–10. That story may be found in* The Lectionary Story Bible, Year B *on pages 226–227.*

Mary was unhappy. She was worried. She was very afraid.

Mary was pregnant. She was going to have a baby. And she was very glad about the baby because of a dream. At least to Mary, it seemed like a dream.

Or maybe it wasn't a dream. Maybe it was real.

Whatever it was, Mary knew that an angel had told her the baby was going to be very special. The baby was going to help show God's love to everyone.

But Mary was also afraid, because in those days people got very angry when a woman had a baby before she was married. Sometimes they got so angry, they threw stones at the woman until they killed her. Mary was happy about the baby, but she was afraid that her family and friends would be very angry at her.

So Mary went to visit her cousin Elizabeth. The angel had told Mary that Elizabeth was also going to have a baby, even though Elizabeth was very old. Much too old to have a baby.

It was a very long walk to Elizabeth's home. But Mary knew Elizabeth would understand. Elizabeth would not be angry.

When Elizabeth saw Mary coming down the path, Elizabeth's baby started moving in her womb. It was almost as if the baby was glad to see Mary coming.

Mary and Elizabeth gave each other a long hug. They cried a little and they laughed. Mary, really just a teenager, and Elizabeth an older woman. And both of them were going to have babies.

After they had talked for a long time, they had something to eat and drink. And then when it was starting to get dark, they sat outside under a tree where it was nice and cool. Mary sang a song for Elizabeth. It was an old song that had been sung many years before by a woman named Hannah.

My heart is so glad,
my heart is so full,
my heart is so wonderfully blessed.

My God has shown love
my God is so strong,
my God cares for those who are poor.

My God feeds the hungry,
my God helps the poor,
my God sends the rich ones away.

God remembers our people,
our families, our friends,
God's promise lives in us today.

Mary stayed with Elizabeth for many days. They talked about their babies. Elizabeth took Mary's hand and held it against her big tummy. Mary could feel the baby moving inside. The two women talked about God, and God's promise of a Chosen One. "I think God has a special dream for both our babies," said Elizabeth.

One day Mary decided to go back home. People might still be angry about her baby, but she felt much stronger after her time with Elizabeth. Mary's friend Joseph still wanted to marry her and to be a father to her baby.

It would still be hard. But Mary could feel God's love. She knew things would be all right.

CHRISTMAS DAY

Jesus Is Born

BASED ON LUKE 2:1–14, (15–20)

Mary's tummy was getting very big. She could feel her baby move inside her. It wouldn't be long before her baby would be born.

Then one day Joseph came in from his shop where he made furniture for people. "Bad news, Mary!" he said. "The soldiers came and told me all of us have to go to the place where we were born. They want to count how many people live in Israel."

"But you were born in Bethlehem," said Mary. "That's a long way from Nazareth."

"I know. And it is going to be even harder for you, because our baby is almost ready to be born."

"Do we have to go?" asked Mary. Joseph nodded, yes.

"Then let's get ready," sighed Mary. "I hope the baby isn't born while we are on the road."

So Mary and Joseph packed clothes and some food. And some clothes for the baby that Mary could feel moving in her womb.

It was a long walk. Sometimes Mary rode on the donkey, but that made her feel sick. "Please, baby," Mary said to herself. "Please don't come till we get to Bethlehem, where we can find a nice warm room to stay in."

But when they got to Bethlehem, there was no room. The whole town was crowded with other people who had come to be counted. Joseph knocked on many doors, but nobody had any room for them.

"The best I could find was in the place where they keep the animals," said Joseph. "It isn't very clean. And it's smelly. But at least the cold wind won't blow on us."

Mary began to cry. She felt so very, very tired, and she knew the baby was ready to be born. "Well, let's go. Now! We have to hurry! The baby is starting to come!"

Joseph helped Mary lie down, gently, on the straw beside the animals. It hurt when the baby was being born. Mary cried. She wanted her mother to be with her. Sometimes she even screamed, it hurt so much.

But then the baby came, and Joseph held it tenderly in his arms. He found some warm water and washed the baby clean.

And that's how the baby Jesus came to be born in a place where only animals were usually born. Mary smiled when Joseph gave the baby to her. A little while later, when Mary put the baby up to her breast, little Jesus began to suck, and Joseph smiled too. They felt happy, even though they were both very tired.

A few hours later, they heard some people talking outside. Then a man walked in the door. He looked around as if he was very mixed up.

When he saw Joseph and Mary and Jesus, he walked over to them. His eyes opened really wide. "Is this God's Chosen One?" he asked.

Mary and Joseph looked at each other. Then at the man. "Yes," said Joseph. "But how did you know?"

"We were up in the fields, looking after our sheep. It was the middle of the night." The shepherd stopped. His mouth opened a few times, but no words came out. He was trying to talk about something that was so wonderful, he couldn't find the right words to tell about it.

"There were bright things, all over the sky!" he said after a while. "And there was music, all around us! Some of the shepherds said it was angels singing!" The shepherd looked at little Jesus. "Can I bring my friends in to see?"

Joseph looked at Mary. She nodded.

The shepherd went to the door and called to his friends. "Come in! Come in and see this wonderful child!"

Five more people came in through the door. One of them was just a boy. He walked right up to the baby. "Could I hold him?" he asked.

Mary smiled at him. "I think it would be better if I held him," she said. "But come close and you can see his face."

The boy came close. The baby opened his eyes. "Oh," said the boy. "He has dark eyes, just like mine. What is his name?"

"His name is Jesus," said Mary.

The boy grinned from ear to ear. "That's my name too!" he grinned. "That's my name too!"

"And do you know what the name Jesus means?" asked Mary

"It means..." The boy looked around at his father. "It means 'God will save us' doesn't it?" He looked at his father again, who smiled and nodded.

Mary and Joseph also smiled.

"Come," the shepherd said to his son. "Little Jesus and his parents are very tired and they need to rest. And we have to go back to look after our sheep."

FIRST SUNDAY AFTER CHRISTMAS DAY

Jesus Goes to the Temple

BASED ON LUKE 2:41–52
WITH REFERENCES TO 1 SAMUEL 2:18–20, 26 AND PSALM 148

Note to leaders and parents: *The custom of the bar mitzvah may not have been observed in Jesus' time. Scholars are not agreed on that point. I included a reference to Jesus' bar mitzvah because it helps place Jesus in the Jewish tradition, and offers an opportunity for modern children to learn a bit about Judaism.*

There are no stories in the Bible that tell about Jesus when he was a child.

The Bible tells us about how Jesus was born. But it doesn't tell us what kinds of games he played with his friends. It doesn't tell us whether Jesus went to school. The Bible doesn't tell us if Jesus' parents ever made him take a "time out" because he did something bad.

But the Bible does tell us about something that happened when Jesus was almost a teenager.

"You are 12 years old, Jesus," Joseph said to him. "That means you are almost a grown-up."

But Jesus still liked to play with his friends. There was no beard growing on his chin. His voice was still high. "I don't feel like a grown-up!" he said to Mary, his mother.

Mary gave her son a hug. "You don't have to grow up any faster than you want to," she said. "You are just beginning your time as a grown-up. You will be an adult for many years, so you can take your time."

"But we want you to come to Jerusalem with us," said Joseph. "It is time for you to get ready for your bar mitzvah next year when you are 13."

Bar mitzvah means "a child of God's promise." When the ceremony is for a girl, it is called a bat mitzvah. It means that the child starts to become a grown-up, and needs to learn how to live God's way.

Jesus was excited about going to Jerusalem. "Wow!" he yelled. "Wowee!! I get to go to the big city!"

It was a long, hard walk from Jesus' home in Nazareth to Jerusalem. But it was kind of fun. They walked with lots of aunts and uncles and cousins, and many of Jesus' friends who were the same age. "Hey, half the town of Nazareth is going," Jesus grinned.

And they sang. Walking is always easier when people sing together. Jesus especially liked one of the songs that was called, “Praise Our God.” One person would sing out a line and then the others would sing it.

“Praise God with the sound of a trumpet,” Mary sang out.

“Praise God with the sound of a trumpet,” everyone sang.

“Let all the stars at night praise God,” Joseph sang out.

“Let all the stars at night praise God,” everyone sang.

“Let all wild animals praise our God,” sang Jesus, in his high, clear voice.

“Let all wild animals praise our God,” everyone sang. Joseph gave Jesus a friendly little poke. He knew how much Jesus liked the animals.

Jesus grinned. He was very happy. He was going to Jerusalem with his family to celebrate the Passover. Passover is the time each year when all Jewish people have a very special meal to remember how God helped their ancestors leave Egypt, where they were slaves.

Jesus, just like all his friends from Nazareth, really liked hearing that old, old story. They especially liked the different kinds of food eaten during the Passover meal. Each part of the dinner helped them remember part of the story.

Then all of them went to the Temple. The Temple was like a very big church and people came from many places to pray there. Jesus and his family and all their friends prayed in the Temple.

"Thank you, God, for all the good things you have done for us. Please help us to be kind and gentle people, and teach us how to live the way you want us to live."

Then it was time to go back home. All of them felt a little sad because they had such a good time.

When Mary and Joseph started walking home, they didn't worry because Jesus wasn't with them. "He's walking with some of his friends," said Mary. But after they had been walking for a while, Mary started to worry. "I'm going to go check to make sure Jesus is walking with his friends," she said to Joseph.

Soon she came running back. "Joseph!" she yelled. "Jesus isn't with his friends. He isn't anywhere in our group. He must be back in Jerusalem!"

"Then we have to go back and find him," said Joseph. "Let's hurry! Something bad might have happened to him!"

Mary and Joseph ran all the way back to Jerusalem. They looked and looked and looked. They couldn't find Jesus anywhere.

"Let's go check with the priests at the Temple," said Joseph. "Maybe they know where he is."

"How would I know where your son is?" said a priest who was standing at the door of the Temple. "That's your job as parents – to look after your children."

"I know. I know," Mary cried. "But have you seen a boy about 12 years old around anywhere."

"Well, there's a boy about 12 years old in that room over there. He's been in there for hours talking with the scribes and the priests and..."

Before the priest could finish speaking, Mary and Joseph were running toward the place where the priest had pointed.

And there he was.

Jesus was sitting and talking with a group of priests and scribes. Some of the smartest people in the country were there. They were talking about God, and Jesus was right there talking with them, even though he was only 12.

Mary was surprised at first, and happy. But then she felt angry. "Jesus!" she said. "We've been looking all over for you! Why didn't you come with your friends and family? We were half sick and worried about you."

Then Jesus walked over to his mother and took her hand. He said something that didn't sound at all like a boy. "I'm sorry I made you worried, Mother," he said. "But didn't you know that I had to be here. I had to be here because God wanted me to be here."

That night when Mary and Joseph were in bed waiting to fall asleep, they talked about Jesus. "He's a strange boy," said Mary. "A wonderfully strange boy."

"I think he's more than a boy now," said Joseph. "There's a part of him that is very grown-up. It scares me a little."

"I keep thinking of Hannah and her son, Samuel," said Mary. "Have you heard that story?"

"Oh yes," said Joseph. "I've heard the priest tell that old, old story many times. You think Jesus is a little like Samuel?"

"I think he's a *lot* like Samuel," said Mary. "Samuel became a prophet. Samuel did God's work and he loved God deeply, all his life. I think Jesus is going to do that too!"

"A prophet? Not everyone likes a prophet." Joseph was quiet for a long time. Then he took Mary's hand. "I think that's wonderful and I think that's scary."

"Yeah. Me too!" said Mary.

The Magi Visit Jesus

BASED ON MATTHEW 2:1–12

Note to leaders and parents: *The readings for Epiphany Sunday are the same in all three years of the* Revised Common Lectionary. *Here we include only the story of the Magi, which you can also find in the* Lectionary Story Bible, Years A and B. *The reading from Isaiah is included in the* Lectionary Story Bible, Year B, *on page 39.*

After Jesus was born, Mary and Joseph stayed in Bethlehem for quite a while. They were waiting for Mary to feel stronger and for Jesus to get a little bigger before they went back to their home in Nazareth. Being born is very hard work for both the mother and the baby.

In a country far away, a bright star shone in the sky. Some Magi saw the star. Magi are sometimes called "wise men," or "wise ones," or "kings."

"That bright star means something important is happening," said one of the Magi. "It's happening in a faraway land. We should go and see."

"Yes," said one of the other Magi. "When a bright star appears in the sky, it means that a king is born."

So they loaded food and clothes onto their camels. Then they started off. As they walked along, the star seemed to move ahead of them. "I think the star is leading us somewhere," said one of the Magi.

So they followed the star. It led them to Jerusalem. In Jerusalem, they went to see King Herod. "We have been following a bright star. We think the star is leading us to a new king who has just been born. Do you know where that king is? We brought him some gifts."

Herod began to feel afraid. Would this baby become king instead of him? Herod was very smart and didn't tell anyone he was afraid. Instead, he just smiled and said to the Magi, "I'll find out for you."

Then he left the Magi and called together all the smart people he knew. He asked them, "Do you know where this new king was born?

"Sure we know. We have some old books that tell us these things. If a new king was born, it would have been in the town of Bethlehem."

Herod went back to the Magi. He smiled nicely to hide his fear.

"The new king was born in Bethlehem," he told them. "Isn't that wonderful? Why don't you go and find him? Give him your gifts and then come back and tell me where he is. I want to take him some gifts, too."

"We'll do that," said the Magi. "Thanks for your help."

So they went to Bethlehem, which isn't very far from Jerusalem. They gave Jesus the special gifts they had brought with them – shining gold, sweet-smelling incense, and a perfume called myrrh.

That night, one of the Magi had a dream. A really bad dream. He shook the other Magi and said, "Wake up! I had a dream that King Herod wants to hurt the baby Jesus. We must not go back to tell Herod where the baby is. We have to go back home, but we should take a different road that doesn't go by Herod's castle. We've got to leave right now!"

FIRST SUNDAY AFTER THE EPIPHANY
(BAPTISM OF JESUS)

Throw Your Money in the River

BASED ON ACTS 8:4–25

Note to leaders and parents: *The prescribed lectionary reading from Acts 8 includes only verses 14–17, which are part of a longer story that begins with verse 4. I tell the entire story here, beginning with verse 4 and ending with verse 25.*

Simon lived in a small place called Samaria. It wasn't very far from the city of Jerusalem.

This was the time after Jesus was killed, and after he had become alive again in a new way. During that time, Jesus talked to many of his friends in Jerusalem. "Please tell my story to as many people as you can. Tell them how much God loves them, and how God's Spirit can make them strong and happy."

Philip, one of Jesus' friends, went to Samaria where Simon lived. But Simon did not like him.

"Philip tells everybody about Jesus," Simon said. "Before he came, everybody liked to watch me do magic tricks. They even paid me money to do my magic tricks. And when I talked, everyone listened. Now they only want to hear Philip tell stories about Jesus."

Philip kept on telling stories about Jesus. The people of Samaria listened. Simon tried hard not to listen. But he couldn't help it.

The people of Samaria said to Philip, "We like your stories. We know that Jesus was God's Chosen One. So we would like to be baptized."

The next day the people of Samaria gathered beside the river. One by one, Philip baptized them. He held them under the water for just a moment. "God, please send your Spirit into Anna," or "God, please send your Spirit into Andrew." And when each one of them had been baptized, they felt clean on the outside of their bodies, and clean on the inside too. They could begin to live as God's friends.

"No way!" said Simon. "I will not let Philip baptize me. No way!"

But as he watched Philip baptize each person, he wanted more and more to be baptized too. So when all the others had been baptized, Simon came up to Philip. "Will you baptize me too?" he asked.

So Philip held Simon under the water for just a moment. "God, please send

your Spirit into Simon." Then Philip brought him up out of the water.

Simon just stood there. He was wet all over, but there were tears coming out of his eyes and a smile on his face. "I feel clean on the outside, and clean on the inside."

After Philip had baptized the people of Samaria, he sent a letter to Jesus' friends in Jerusalem. "The people of Samaria have been baptized," said the letter. "But they haven't received God's Spirit. Can Peter and John come and lay their hands on the people here, so that they can have God's Spirit too?"

So Peter and John walked over from Jerusalem. This time Simon was first in the line. "Please lay your hands on me!" he said. "I want to have God's Spirit in me."

So Peter and John put their hands on Simon's head and shoulders. "Please, God, send the Holy Spirit into Simon, who is your friend. Make him strong and happy."

Then Peter and John did that for the other people of Samaria who had been baptized by Philip. They all felt happy and strong and full of God's Spirit.

Then Simon got a funny look on his face. "Peter," he whispered, so nobody else could hear. "Will you teach me how to do that? How to put my hands on people so they can get God's Spirit. I'll give you a lot of money if you do that!"

Peter looked right at Simon. Peter was angry. "You can throw your money in the river!" he said to Simon. "God doesn't want your money! You can't buy God's Spirit with money!"

"I, I'm sorry, I..." Simon didn't know what to say.

"Go find a quiet place to pray, Simon," said Peter. "Tell God you are sorry for trying to buy the Holy Spirit."

That's how Simon learned that God doesn't care about money. "I will go and pray and I will tell God I am sorry," said Simon. Then he looked at Peter. "Will you pray for me too?"

Peter smiled at Simon. "Yes, Simon," he said. "I will pray for you. Oh, and Simon..."

"Yes?"

Peter gave Simon a little hug. "God loves you very much," he said.

FIRST SUNDAY AFTER THE EPIPHANY
(BAPTISM OF JESUS)

Jesus Is Baptized

BASED ON LUKE 3:15–17, 21–22

People came from all over. "Let's go hear John!" they said to each other.

Some of them walked a long way. Some of the people came just because they thought it would be fun to hear John talking. "He's a little bit weird," they laughed. "He wears animal skins for clothes and he shouts and yells."

But other people came because they were hungry for God. They felt kind of empty inside and they thought maybe John could help them. They wanted to be baptized. "When we are baptized by John, we won't feel empty anymore," they said. "We'll know that God lives inside us."

All the people gathered beside the Jordan River where John was speaking. "Get ready!" said John. "I baptize you with water, but someone is coming – God is sending us someone – someone who will baptize you with God's Holy Spirit."

As each person came to be baptized, John held them under the water for just a moment and prayed, "Please, God, fill this person with your love."

One of the people who came to be baptized was Jesus. And when he had been baptized, Jesus stood in the water for a long time praying.

As he was praying, it seemed as if the sky opened. It seemed as if God's Spirit came down to Jesus, in the shape of a pure, white bird – a dove.

And there was a voice – a soft and beautiful voice that said, "You are my child. I love you. I am pleased with you."

Many Different Kinds of People

BASED ON 1 CORINTHIANS 12:1–11

"I am Jesus' friend," said Paul. "I never met Jesus before he died, but the Spirit of Jesus came to me in a very special way."

Paul went to many places telling people about Jesus. And he wrote lots of letters. He wrote them a long time ago, after the time when Jesus was alive again.

Here is part of one letter Paul wrote to the people who were in the church at Corinth. You can find both of the letters to the Corinthians in the Bible.

Dear sisters and brothers in Corinth:

Always remember that each one of us is different. No two people are alike. Some people are good at doing one thing, and others can do something else. But it is God's Spirit that helps them do those things.

Some people are really good at helping us to be fair and kind to each other. God's Spirit works through them to help us know that we are all part of God's family.

Some people help us understand why sometimes we get along nicely with each other, and sometimes we argue. We even fight sometimes. God's Spirit works through those people to help us understand our feelings.

Some people have good memories. They can remember directions – they can remember the words they read in a book – they can remember how to do things. God's Spirit works through them to help people remember things.

Some people know how to help when someone isn't feeling well. God's Spirit works through them to help people when they are sick.

People can do many different things. But it's God's Spirit that helps them do those things. Each person is different, but every one of them is able to do something important because the Spirit of God helps them do their best.

The Wonderful Wedding Party

BASED ON JOHN 2:1–11

One day, Jesus and his mother were invited to a wedding in a town called Cana. Two of their friends were getting married, and they were having a big party to celebrate.

It was a wonderful wedding. The bride and the groom were all dressed up in their best clothes. The rabbi of the synagogue, who is like the minister of a church, asked them some important questions.

"Will you love and care for each other? Will you share with each other and be kind and gentle?" The bride and the groom both said, "Yes, we will."

There was a lot of good food at the wedding. There was meat, and there was bread. There were nuts and there were nice juicy figs. And good sweet wine to drink.

Then Mary, Jesus' mother, noticed a problem. "They have no more wine!" she said to Jesus.

"That's their problem, Mother," Jesus said. "It's not our problem."

But Mary knew that Jesus would be able to do something. So she said to one of the helpers who had been serving the wine. "Just do what Jesus tells you."

After a little while, Jesus sighed. "Well, all right. I guess I can help." Jesus pointed to six big empty jars. "Fill those up with water," he said to one of the helpers.

That's what they did.

"Now take a large jug and fill it from one of those jars. And pour it into people's cups."

As people began to taste what the helpers had poured into their cups, they looked surprised. "Wow! This is really good wine! Where did you get it?"

The helpers knew, but they didn't say anything. And of course, Jesus and his mother knew.

But nobody else knew. "This is just great," one of the guests said to the bride and groom. "Usually people serve the best wine first. But this is the best wine yet, and you have served it last. What a wonderful party!"

THIRD SUNDAY AFTER THE EPIPHANY

Going Home

BASED ON NEHEMIAH 8:1–3, 5–6, 8–10

Many, many years before the time of Jesus, the Hebrew people felt very sad. The king of Persia brought a big army. His army fought the Hebrew army and beat them. Then the king made the Hebrews go back with him to his faraway country. And they had to work for the people of Persia.

When the king of Persia died, his son became the king. He was much more kind than his father. He didn't want to hurt the Hebrews.

The king had a Hebrew servant named Nehemiah. "My people are very sad. They miss their home," Nehemiah said to the king. "They would like to be able to pray to God in their temple at Jerusalem."

"That's a good idea, Nehemiah," said the king. "Gather all the Hebrews who would like to go back to their home. Take them back to Israel."

"Thank you," said Nehemiah. "Your father's soldiers broke down the walls of our city, Jerusalem, and they destroyed the temple where we pray to our God. May we fix the walls and rebuild the temple?"

"That's a good idea," said the king. "And I will help you."

So Nehemiah and many Hebrew people walked all the way from Persia back to their home in Israel.

When they got to Jerusalem, they started to work. It was very hard work fixing the walls of Jerusalem. They had to carry many heavy stones and build new gates. And they had to fix their temple so they would have a place to pray to God.

Those who had strong muscles lifted the big stones. Those who knew how to cut stones with chisels made the stones nice and smooth. Those who knew how to cook made food for all the workers. Some of the children carried water to the workers, because the sun was very hot. And they all worked together.

When it was all done, Nehemiah asked the people to gather in one place. They sat down on the ground because they were tired from their hard work. But they were happy.

"Listen," said Nehemiah in a very loud voice so everyone could hear. "Listen to Ezra, who is one of our teachers. Listen to him read some words that we believe came to us from God. Listen carefully!"

Then Ezra stood up on a platform they had built. He slowly unrolled a scroll. When the people saw Ezra do this, they knew he was going to read something very important. So they all stood up.

"Dear God," said Ezra, "help us listen to these words. Help us understand what the words mean, so that we can live God's way."

All the people smiled and said, "Amen! Amen!" Which means, "Yes, Yes, that's the way we want it to be."

Then Ezra read from the book. The book told the story of how God helped Moses lead the ancestors of the Hebrew people out of Egypt, and how God had sent special people called "prophets" to help people learn about God.

"Now God has brought us back to our own country," said Ezra. "We fixed up our city of Jerusalem and we have a new temple where we can pray to God. We should say thank you to God who helped us do all this!"

So all the people smiled at each other. "Thank you, God!" they said. "Thank you, God, for bringing us back to our own country and our own Temple."

"So let us always remember this special time," said Ezra. "Let's remember this story and tell it to our children, so they can tell it to their children.

"And do you know what God wants us to do right now?" asked Ezra.

"What?"

"God wants us to be happy. This is a happy time, so sing and dance and laugh and eat some really great food. This is a special time. Feel God's joy inside you. When you can feel God's joy inside you, you will be strong."

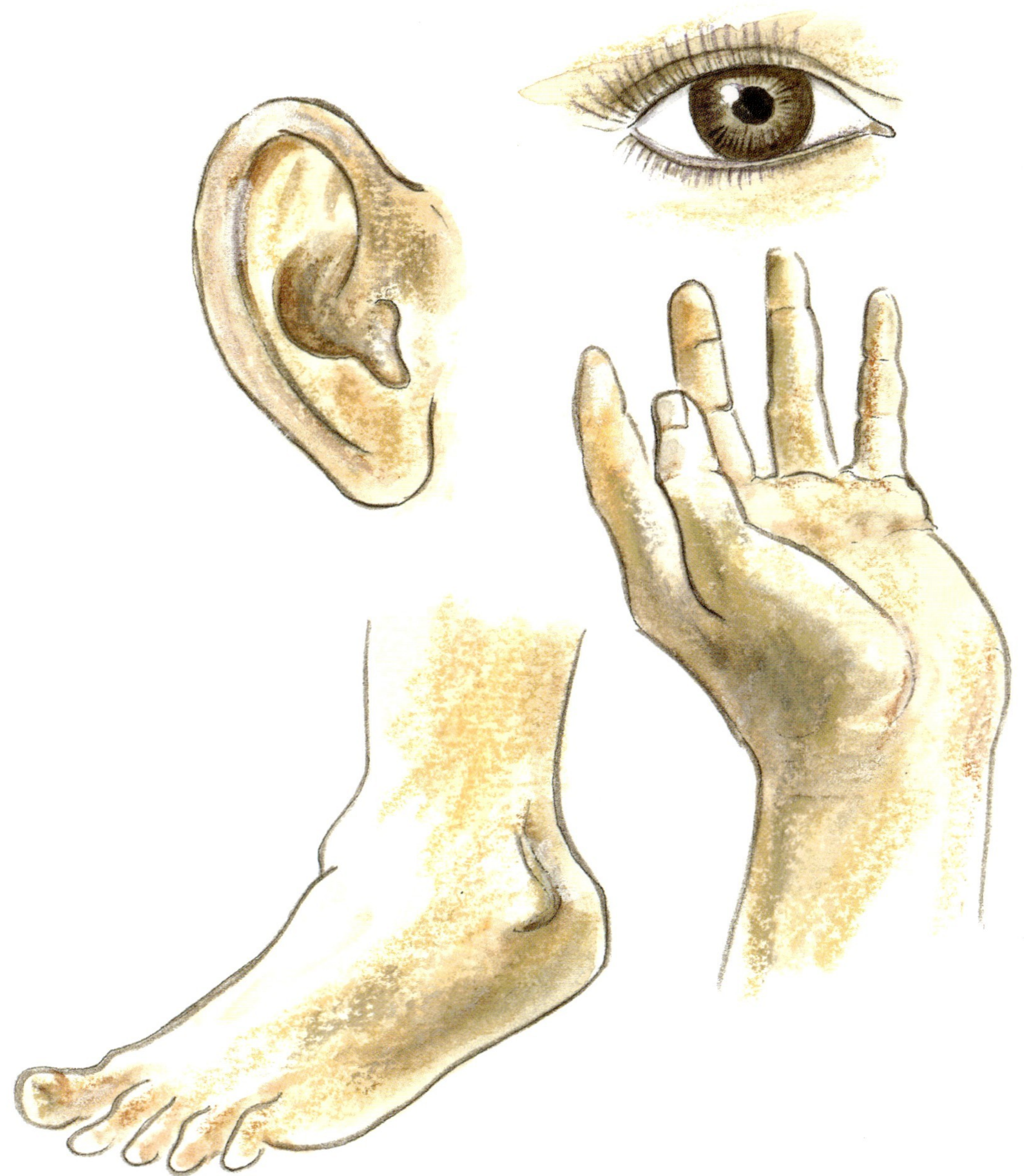

Each Person Is Important

BASED ON 1 CORINTHIANS 1:10, 12:4–31

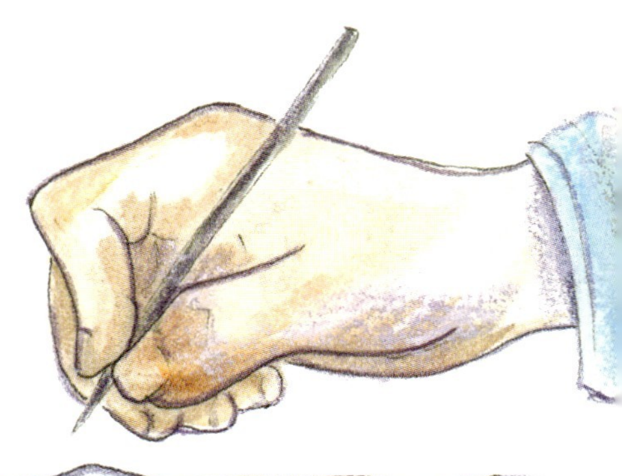

Here is part of a letter Paul wrote. He wrote it to people in Corinth who sometimes argued with each other. Paul wanted them to stop their fighting and work together. He wanted them to know that God thinks every single person is important.

Dear friends in Corinth:

Please try to get along! Jesus doesn't want you to be arguing. Jesus doesn't want you to be angry. Jesus wants you to be kind to each other. Jesus wants you to be friends.

We all like to have things our own way. Everyone would like to be boss over everybody else. But you are part of a Christian church. You must work together if you want to live in God's way.

Think of your church as if it is a person's body. The whole church body should live in God's way. Not just some parts of it.

Would your foot say, "Because I am not a hand, I don't belong to the body"?

That's silly!

Would your ear say, "Because I am not an eye, I don't belong to the body"?

That's silly!

If your whole body were an eye, how would you hear things?

If your whole body were an ear, how would you smell things?

Your eye can't say to your hand, "I don't need you." That's silly.

Your head can't say to your feet, "I don't need you." That's silly.

God has put all the parts of our body together so that they help each other. Everything is part of one body.

If part of your body is hurting, then you feel bad all over.

If part of your body is happy, you feel good all over.

The church is like the body of Christ. Each one of us is like the hands, or feet, or eyes, or ears of that body.

Each one of us can do different things. Some people can sing. Others can listen. A few can run fast. Some people can work hard. Others can draw nice pictures. Some people can think and talk about important things.

Each one of us is important. We are Christ's body and we are all needed. Living in God's way means working together as the church.

Your friend,
Paul

Jesus Learns about His Job

BASED ON LUKE 4:14–21

Jesus walked to many different places to tell people about God. He told them stories and he often helped people who were sick.

One day, Jesus went back to the town of Nazareth where he grew up. He went to the synagogue, the place where people gather to pray to God and to study God's word.

"Why don't you read something to us," said his family and friends. "Find the part of the Bible that we are supposed to think about today, and read it to us."

So Jesus took the big scroll, the one that had the words written by the prophet Isaiah. This is what Jesus read:

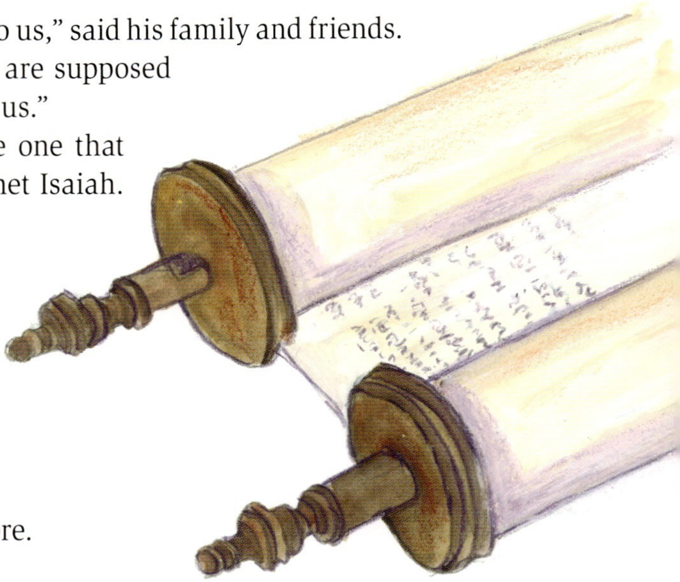

> The Spirit of God is inside me
> because God has chosen me
> to tell poor people about God's love.
> God has sent me,
> to tell people in prison
> that they aren't prisoners anymore.
> God has sent me
> to tell blind people that they can see,
> and to tell everyone
> that God is with them,
> around them, inside them.

When Jesus finished reading from the scroll, he rolled it back up. Then he looked at the people in the synagogue.

"The prophet Isaiah wrote that many years ago," said Jesus. "But God wants you to hear those words, right here. Right now. And God wants me to hear those words too. Because I think the prophet Isaiah was talking about me and what I must do with my life."

Jeremiah Becomes a Prophet

BASED ON JEREMIAH 1:4–10

Jeremiah didn't really want to be a prophet.

A prophet is like a minister in a church. Or like a person who helps us keep our world safe and clean. A prophet tells us what God wants us to know.

Jeremiah didn't want to do that. "Being a prophet is hard work," he said to himself. "And, often, people don't like what the prophets tell them."

Then Jeremiah had a vision. A vision is like a dream that happens when you are awake. In the vision, God spoke to Jeremiah.

"Even before you were born," Jeremiah heard God say, "even when you were just beginning to grow inside your mother's tummy, I wanted you to be a prophet."

"No," said Jeremiah. "I don't want to stand up and talk to the people. I'm just a child. I don't know how to do that. I'm afraid to be a prophet!"

"You are not too young," God said. "And you don't need to be afraid because I will be with you all the time. I will help you be a prophet. I will help you find the right words to say."

And then, in his vision, Jeremiah felt God touch his lips. Very gently.

"Now I have put my words into your mouth," Jeremiah heard God say. "Now go out and tell people how to live God's way. You will teach people how to be kind to each other, and to our world. You are now my messenger, Jeremiah."

Then the vision stopped. Jeremiah rubbed his eyes. "Was that really God talking to me?" he wondered. "Was it really God who touched my lips?"

Jeremiah knew it was.

He was still a little afraid of being a prophet. "But that's what God wants me to be," Jeremiah said to himself. "So I will try to be the best prophet I can be."

Paul's Song about Love

BASED ON 1 CORINTHIANS 13:1–13

In one of the letters that Paul wrote to the people who lived in Corinth, he wanted to tell them about love. What does it mean when we say that we love someone? Paul wrote a song about love. Here are some of the words for the song.

If I talk like an angel
but I don't have love,
I am nothing.

If I talk like a prophet,
if I give away my money,
but I don't have love,
I am nothing.

Love is good.
Love is kind.
And love will never end.

Prophets will stop talking,
teachers will stop teaching,
but love will never end.

When I was a baby,
I spoke like a baby,
I thought like a baby.
But now I am growing.
I'm not a baby anymore
and I know how to love.

So God gives us faith
and God gives us hope
and God gives us love.

But the best thing of all,
is love.

Isaiah Becomes a Prophet

BASED ON ISAIAH 6:1–8

Old Isaiah was a prophet. He tried his very best to help people live God's way. "Please listen to what God is telling you," he would say.

Old Isaiah had many friends, but his best friends were children. He loved all the children and liked to talk with them. He tried to play games with them sometimes. But he could only move slowly.

"My poor bones," he said. "They are too old." Then Old Isaiah would make big puffing noises and sit down again.

Old Isaiah loved all the children, but he was best friends with Rebekah. Rebekah came to see him every day. Old Isaiah always smiled when he saw her coming. His smile was so big, she could see all his teeth, except where he didn't have any.

Sometimes Rebekah would go with Old Isaiah to the marketplace. He would sit on a rock in the middle of the market and talk to anyone who would listen.

There were always lots of people in the marketplace. Some of them paid no attention to Old Isaiah. Some would yell angry words at him. But some of the people would stop and listen.

One day at the marketplace, some people were very angry at Old Isaiah. "You mind your own business!" they yelled. "We don't want to live God's way. We just want to get lots of money."

Old Isaiah walked very slowly as he and Rebekah went home from the marketplace. She could tell he felt very sad.

"Do you like being a prophet?" she asked.

"Mostly, yes. But sometimes, like today, I wish I was somebody else."

"Do you have to be a prophet?" Rebekah asked.

"Yes."

"Why?"

"Because God asked me to be a prophet," said Old Isaiah.

"Did God just come and talk to you?" asked Rebekah.

Old Isaiah stopped walking. There was a faraway remembering look in his eyes. "It happened when I was still a young man," said Old Isaiah. "I had a vision. I saw it all in my mind. Like a dream, except that I was awake."

"Did you really see God?" asked Rebekah.

"Yes. In my mind I saw God." Old Isaiah sat down on a rock beside the path.

"I saw God sitting on a throne. And there were angels there with God."

"What do angels look like?" Rebekah's eyes were wide open.

"Angels look like..." Old Isaiah scratched his head. "Angels look like angels. And they were singing and shouting back and forth to each other. They sang, 'Holy, holy, holy is God. God's love fills the whole earth.'"

"Were you afraid?" asked Rebekah. "I sure would be."

"Yes, I was afraid. And that's what I said to God. 'I'm not a good person, God. And I often say and do bad things. Awful things. And the people I live with are like that too.'

"Then one of the angels took a pair of tongs and got a red-hot piece of coal from the fire. The angel came and touched my lips with the burning coal. I thought it would hurt terribly but it didn't. And then the angel talked to me. 'Now your mouth is ready to speak my words,' said the angel. 'You are ready. Just remember, God loves you.'"

Old Isaiah stopped talking. His eyes were closed. Rebekah didn't say anything. She knew her friend would tell the rest of the story when he was ready.

Old Isaiah took a deep breath. "Then I heard God's voice. God's voice! I heard God's voice say to me, 'I need someone to go and talk to the people. I need someone to teach them how to live God's way. Who shall I send?'"

"What did you say?" Rebekah whispered. She took the old man's hand.

"I said..." Old Isaiah's voice was so soft Rebekah had to move up really close to hear. "I said, 'Here I am. Send me.'"

Rebekah had tears in her eyes. So did Old Isaiah.

Sometimes when things are truly wonderful – truly beautiful – sometimes when we feel so full of God's love, it brings tears to our eyes.

FIFTH SUNDAY AFTER THE EPIPHANY

Simon Gets a New Job

BASED ON LUKE 5:1–11

Simon was tired. He was cleaning his fishing net on the shore. He had been fishing all night long. But there didn't seem to be any fish.

He saw Jesus and a crowd of people walking toward him.

"Simon," called Jesus. "May I use your boat?"

"Sure," said Simon. "Why?"

"If you anchor it near the shore, I can sit in your boat and talk to the people."

So Jesus sat in Simon's boat. Jesus told the people about God's promise to love everyone. Simon listened too.

When Jesus was finished talking to the people, he asked Simon, "How many fish did you catch?"

"There aren't any fish out there," Simon grumbled.

"Sure there are," laughed Jesus. "Get back into your boat and go where the water is deep. Then try again."

"Wow!" shouted Simon after he put the nets back in the water. "Look at all these fish. My boat is full. Look out! It might sink."

It was hard to row that boat full of fish back to the shore. As he rowed, Simon thought about Jesus. He thought about the things he had just heard Jesus saying.

Then Simon felt sad. "I can't live in God's way," he thought. "I tell lies. I get angry. I'm ugly. I do stupid things. Jesus wouldn't want to be my friend."

Jesus was standing on the shore waiting for Simon. "Simon," said Jesus, "I'd like to talk to you."

"You shouldn't be talking to me," Simon said to Jesus. "I'm not a good person. I do bad things. And I'm not very smart."

"Simon," said Jesus. "I helped you with your work. Why don't you come and help me with mine?"

"But all I can do is catch fish!"

"Fine," laughed Jesus. "Come, help me catch people."

That's how Simon became one of Jesus' special helpers. Other women and men also became Jesus' special helpers. The Bible calls them "disciples."

FIFTH SUNDAY AFTER THE EPIPHANY

Happy People

BASED ON PSALM 1 AND JEREMIAH 17:5–10

Here's a song that comes from two places in the Bible – the book of Psalms and the book of Jeremiah. Jesus liked to sing songs like this one. We don't have the music, but you could make up your own music to go with these words.

Happy people
don't listen to those
who hurt or kill other people.

Happy people
don't listen to those
who say mean things about others.

Happy people
do listen to those
who smile and talk about God.

Happy people
do listen to those
who love the world that God loves.

Happy people
are like fresh green trees
that grow near the water,
that bloom in the springtime,
that grow good fruit we can eat.

SIXTH SUNDAY AFTER THE EPIPHANY

Jesus Teaches

BASED ON LUKE 6:17–23

Many people came to hear Jesus teach. Sometimes crowds of people came. They followed Jesus wherever he went. Here are some of the things Jesus said about growing in God's way. They are sometimes called "Beatitudes," which means "to be blessed" or "to be happy."

If you feel very small inside,
be happy.
Gods love is yours.

If you feel very sad inside,
be happy.
God will help you feel better.

If you think you are not very smart,
be happy.
God has a promise for you.

If you try very hard to be good,
be happy.
God will help you feel good inside.

If you really care about other people,
be happy.
God cares about you.

If you try hard to work for peace,
be happy.
God says "You are my child."

If people are mean to you because you
love God,
be happy.
You will always be part
of God's family.

SEVENTH SUNDAY AFTER THE EPIPHANY

Jesus Talks about Love

BASED ON LUKE 6:27–38

Jesus often talked about love to his friends. "That's because loving is the most important thing we do," he said to them.

"But who should we love?" asked Mary.

"Yeah," said Peter. "We can't just love everybody."

"We can, Peter. But it's hard," said Jesus. "So why don't we all sit down here on the grass. I'll tell you some things about love."

"Love the people who don't like you," said Jesus. "Love the people who say mean things to you. When you pray to God, talk about those people. Say to God, 'Please help me love them.'

"Suppose someone hits you. Don't hit them back. Be kind to them instead.

"If someone takes something away from you, don't yell and fight. Give them something else.

"Be kind to others, the way you would like them to be kind to you."

"Those are very hard things to do, Jesus!" said Peter.

"I know," said Jesus. "It's easy to love the people who love you. It's easy to love your friends. But God wants you to do more than that – something that is really hard."

"Will God help us love people that are hard to love?" asked Mary.

"For sure," said Jesus. "When someone does something you don't like, try this. Don't do or say anything for a little bit; just breathe in and out a few times. Then, in your mind, ask, 'God, what should I do?' Then breathe in and out a few more times. Then God will put an idea in your head, and that idea may be to go and talk it over with some other people."

Mary and Peter looked at each other. It still seemed impossible.

"Do you know *why* you should do that, Peter?" Jesus looked at his friends. "Do you know *why* you should love like that, Mary?"

Both of them shook their heads. They didn't know.

"Because that is what God does," said Jesus.

"But I thought you said God was sad when someone is mean, or steals something," said Mary.

"Yes," said Jesus. "God is sad, just as you feel sad when someone does something bad. But even when God is sad about the things we do, God keeps on loving us. People do many things that make God sad, but God never stops loving them."

"Is that what you mean when you talk about living God's way?" asked Peter.

"Yes, that's what I mean. It's not an easy thing, but you *can* do it. God gives you so much love, you have lots to share with people who are mean, or who hurt you or steal from you.

"And you know something else?" Jesus looked around at his friends. "When you give away lots and lots of love, you'll find it all comes back to you. When you give love away, you always find you have more love than you started with."

"Does that mean we have to kiss and hug everybody?" asked Peter.

Jesus laughed. "No. Some people don't really like to be hugged and kissed. When you love someone, you think about the good things they do. You do kind things for them whenever you can. You say kind things about them. You try really hard to be their friend."

"But what if they just laugh at you?" asked Peter. "What if they say you're stupid and just walk away. Or maybe they even hit you?"

"I didn't say it was easy," said Jesus. "And it may take a long time – maybe years – before they stop acting that way. But you keep trying. Over and over and over. And it's a good thing to talk to God about it in your prayers. That way you'll become a stronger person each time you show that kind of love."

Isaiah's Beautiful Dream

BASED ON ISAIAH 55:10–13

"You're such a dreamer," Rebekah said to her friend one day.

Old Isaiah shook his head, as if there was something loose inside.

"But that's okay," she said. "I love you even when you say such a strange things."

Old Isaiah smiled and Rebekah could see his teeth. Except where he didn't have any. "My old brain doesn't work very well sometimes," he said. "Sometimes I wonder where all my dreams come from."

Rebekah looked right at Old Isaiah. "Don't say that! You know perfectly well where your dreams come from. You told me yourself that they come from God."

"Yes, oh yes." Old Isaiah closed his eyes again. "But sometimes I think you and I are the only ones who know that my dreams come from God. The people in the marketplace think I'm just a silly old man."

"Never mind," said Rebekah. "You tell me the dream you just had, and then you can write it in your book. Maybe lots of people will read your book and they will believe your dreams."

"Well!" said old Isaiah. He took a big, deep breath. He liked to tell his dreams to Rebekah, because that helped him find words to write about them. "Here's my dream," he said.

> The rain and the snow come down from above.
> They bring water to make the plants grow.
> The rain and the snow grow wheat and fruit.
> They bring food for my people to eat.
>
> And that's how it is with my story, says God.
> That's how it is with the words that I say.
> My words are like rain and snow that give life.
> They're like food for my people to eat.
> And yes, you will walk in peace.
> And yes, you will run and be glad.

And the mountains and hills
will sing you a song,
and the trees will clap their hands.

No more sharp and prickly thorns.
Just big and beautiful trees.
No more dry and ugly weeds.
My words will grow and give life.

EIGHTH SUNDAY AFTER THE EPIPHANY

Jesus Tells Stories

BASED ON LUKE 6:39–49

Jesus liked stories.

When he was a boy living in Nazareth, his mother, Mary, used to tell him many stories. Jesus remembered all those stories. Soon, he found stories of his own.

Some of them were about things that really happened. And some of the stories he just made up in his head.

"But it's funny," Jesus said to his friends one day. "Whether I make up a story in my own head, or whether the story is about something that really happened, I always learn something about God from the story. Or about how to live God's way."

Here are some short stories that Jesus made up in his head.

"One day Timothy looked at his friend Lois. 'You've got a speck of dirt in your eye,' said Timothy. 'Why don't you get it out? You don't look very nice with dirt in your eye.'

"But Lois looked right at Timothy. 'Oh, Timothy,' she said. 'If you could only see yourself. You say I have a bit of dirt in my eye, but you have a great big stick in your own eye!'

"So," said Jesus, "It's always easier to see the bad things in another person, than it is to see what you are like yourself."

"Come over here and look at this tree," said Jesus. "It's a nice tree, isn't it? It has good roots that go down to the water. It has strong branches that catch the warm sunshine. The sunshine makes the leaves big and green and strong.

"But here is another tree. It doesn't have good roots, so it never has enough water. The branches are all broken and rotten.

"There are apples on both trees. But guess which tree has the nicest apples?

"You are like one of those trees. If you learn good things from kind people, you are like a tree that has its roots in the nice, cool water. And if you try to learn about God, if you listen to my stories, then you are like a tree with strong branches and leaves that catch the warm sunshine.

"So," said Jesus, "If you are like that strong, green tree, you will do good things for yourself and for others."

"There were two men. Ezra and Benjamin. They each wanted to build a house.

"Ezra dug down into the ground till he found a big, strong rock for the house to stand on. Then he got the best stones and nice straight boards, so the house was really strong.

"When the winds blew and the water came and washed over the house, it didn't break. It didn't float away. Ezra had made a good, strong house.

"Benjamin also built a house. But he didn't really care what the house was like. He didn't bother putting it on a big strong rock. He just built it on the soft sand. And Benjamin didn't get nice straight boards. He just used some old sticks he found close by. 'That's plenty good enough!' said Benjamin.

"When the winds blew and the water came and washed over the house, it just fell apart. The whole thing just floated away.

"So," said Jesus, "If you listen to my stories, and you try hard to live the way God wants you to live, you are like Ezra who built a good, strong house.

"But if you don't listen to my stories – if you don't really care what you do or who you might hurt – you are like Benjamin. His house fell apart and just floated away."

Abigail Learns about God's Love

BASED ON LUKE 7:1–10

Note to leaders and parents: *The lectionary suggests this passage for both Epiphany 9 and Proper 4. You can find the story I wrote for Proper 4 on page 155.*

Sometimes Jesus said things that people didn't want to hear. One day he was teaching people in a synagogue. A synagogue is like a church.

"God loves everybody," he said to the people in the synagogue. "Not just us Jewish people."

"I don't believe that," said Abigail. "How can God love those wicked Roman soldiers who keep hurting us?"

"Sometimes Roman soldiers do bad things. And that makes God sad," said Jesus. "But God still loves them. Just like God loves you, even when you have done bad things."

"I've never done anything bad!" said Abigail.

Jesus looked at her kind of sideways. She could tell he didn't believe her.

Just then some messengers came to Jesus. "We have a message for you," they said to Jesus. "It's from Antonius. He has a friend who is very sick. Will you come and help him?"

That made Abigail really angry. "Jesus can't go help Antonius!" she yelled. "Antonius is a Roman soldier. Roman soldiers are mean and ugly and stupid and they hurt us all the time."

"That's not true!" said the messengers. "Antonius is a kind person. He even gave us money to build our synagogue."

"You see?" Jesus said to Abigail. "Sometimes Roman soldiers do good things too." Then Jesus turned to the messengers. "Show me the way to Antonius' house."

So Jesus and the messengers started walking down the street. When they were almost at Antonius' house, another messenger came. "Antonius has a message for you, Jesus. He doesn't think he's a very good person. He thinks maybe you wouldn't want to come to his house. But Antonius says that all you have to do is say so, and his friend will get well."

Jesus smiled. He didn't say anything. He just started walking back toward the synagogue. Then another messenger came running.

"Jesus!" he called. "Antonius asked me to tell you. His friend isn't sick anymore. And he wants me to say thank you."

Jesus walked back to the synagogue. "Abigail!" he called. "Come sit beside me. I have something to tell you."

Abigail didn't really want to talk to Jesus. She was still angry at him for going to help a Roman soldier. But she came anyway.

"Abigail," said Jesus. "Antonius is a Roman soldier. But he is also a kind and gentle person, and he tries very hard to live God's way. Sometimes soldiers do bad things. Sometimes soldiers do good things. Just like you, Abigail."

Abigail's face turned red. She looked down at the floor. She knew she had done some bad things, just like everybody else.

Jesus touched Abigail's hand. "God loves you, Abigail, and God loves Antonius. And everybody else, Abigail. *Everyone* else!"

A Smiley, Shiny Face

BASED ON EXODUS 34:29–35

Hannah had been helping her mom all day. And she loved it.

That's because Hannah was now a big sister. Hannah's mom had given birth to a baby. They named the new baby Miriam, because that was the name of her mom's sister, Hannah's Auntie Miriam.

Hannah's mom was still very tired from giving birth to baby Miriam. "That's okay," said Hannah. She gave her mom a big smile and a kiss. "I'm nine years old now, and I can help."

"And you just keep smiling, don't you?" Hannah's mom was laughing a little. "You've been smiling, and smiling and smiling ever since baby Miriam was born."

"I know," said Hannah. She was laughing now too. "My face hurts a little from smiling so much. But I can't help it!"

"Hello!" They heard a voice at the door. It was Auntie Miriam. "Can I come in? Can I come and see the wonderful baby that has my name?"

"Hi Auntie Miriam," said Hannah.

Auntie Miriam picked up baby Miriam. "Isn't she beautiful?"

"She's the most beautiful baby in the whole world!" said Hannah.

"And look at you!" said Auntie Miriam. "You have such a smile on your face, you light up the whole world."

That made Hannah smile even more.

She smiled so hard that little tears came to her eyes.

"Do you know what you and your shiny face remind me of, Hannah?" Auntie Miriam sat down on a stool. She held the baby in one arm, and put her other arm around Hannah.

"You remind me of your Uncle Moses. When he came down from the mountain."

"I remember that," said Hannah's mom. "He was smiling so hard, I thought his ears would fall off! It looked as if his face was shining."

Auntie Miriam and Hannah laughed. "Uncle Moses was smiling so hard because he had been talking with God. He had been up on a mountain for many days, and when he came down you could tell just by looking at him that something wonderful had happened."

"He brought down some big stones with writing on them, didn't he?" said Hannah. "The writing was about rules and stuff."

"That's right," said Auntie Miriam. "We call them commandments. God was telling us about things we should do and things we shouldn't do. Those commandments help us live God's way."

"And Uncle Moses' face was shining just like mine." Hannah started dancing around the room.

"Oh yes, his face was shining," said Auntie Miriam. "He was smiling so hard, people said his face was shining, like a light. 'Cover your face!' they said. So Uncle Moses put a veil over his face."

"Is Uncle Moses' face still shining?" asked Hannah.

"Not all the time. But Uncle Moses has a special place – a tent – where he goes to talk to God. When he is praying, he is talking to God. And every time he comes out of the tent, he puts that veil over his face because his face is shining all over again."

"So you get a shiny, smiley face if you talk to God or your mom gives you a baby sister."

Auntie Miriam laughed and gave Hannah another hug. "Well, your mom can't have a baby sister every day so that you can keep on smiling. But you can talk to God every day. God will help your face shine."

"Should I cover my face?" asked Hannah.

"Oh no, never," laughed Auntie Miriam. "If you have a smiley face – a shiny face – let everyone see it. Then they might start smiling too."

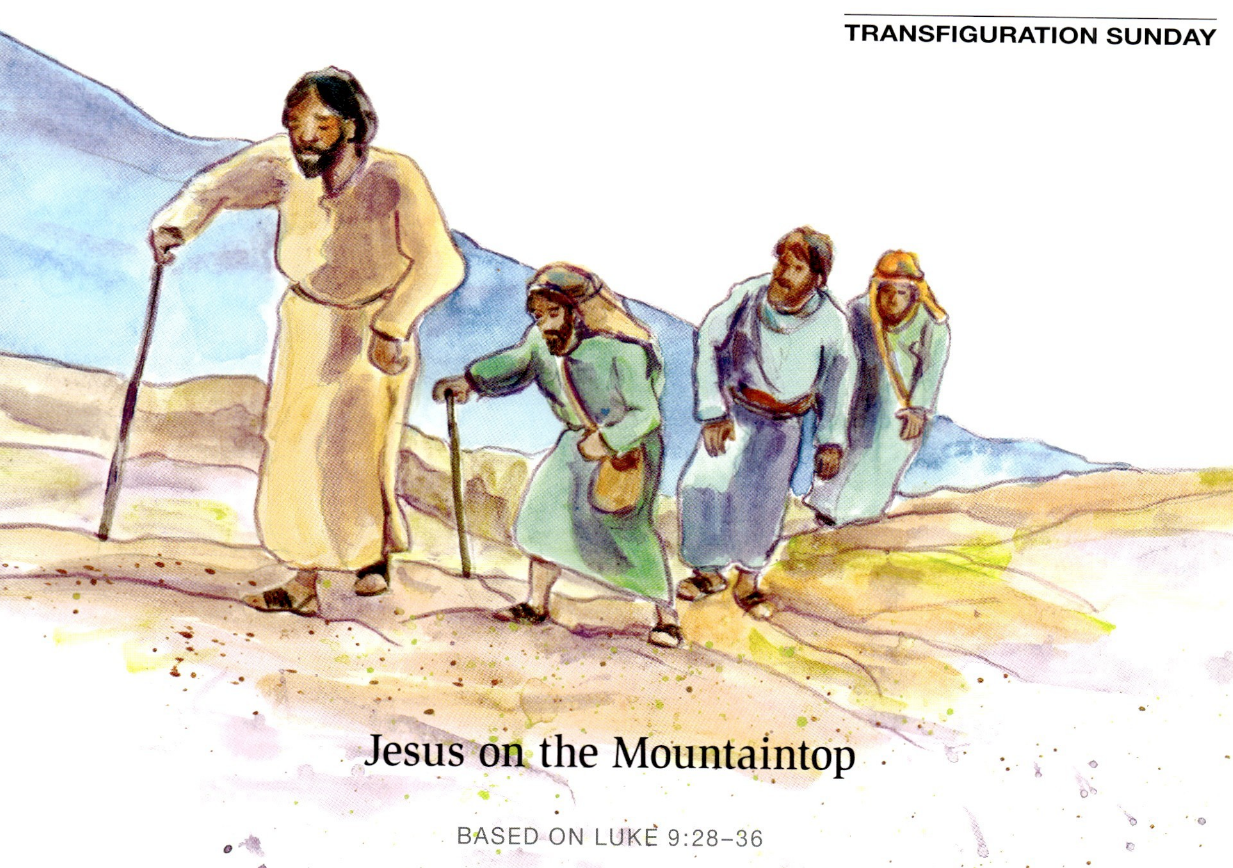

Jesus on the Mountaintop

BASED ON LUKE 9:28–36

"What happened, Peter?" Mark asked.

"I can't tell you. Not now," Peter answered.

"Are you sick? You and James and John. You look so pale!"

"No, we're not sick, Mark." Peter was shaking a little. "Something wonderful happened. But I can't tell you about it. Not now."

Years after Jesus was killed and came back to life, Peter finally told Mark the story.

"Jesus took us to the top of a mountain," said Peter. "It was a long climb. We were tired when we got there."

"Just you and Jesus?" Mark asked.

"No, James and his brother John were there, too. They know what happened.

"I'll never forget that time," said Peter. "All of a sudden, Jesus changed. His face shone. It was like looking into the sun. And his clothes turned white. Really white. Then there were two people with Jesus."

"Who?" Mark asked.

"Elijah and Moses."

"How did you know?"

"I don't know how we knew," said Peter. "But we knew. And Jesus was talking to them."

"So what did you do?" said Mark.

"I didn't know what to do. I said to Jesus, 'Shouldn't we build three little houses here? I could build one for you, one for Moses, and one for Elijah.' It sounds silly, now that I think about it. But I was so afraid. I didn't know what to say!"

"What did Jesus say?" Mark asked.

"He didn't say anything. A bright cloud came and covered him. Then we heard a voice. James and John heard it, too. You can ask them."

"Was it God?"

"It must have been. The voice said, 'This is my Son, my Chosen One. I love him. Listen to him.'"

"That's all?" asked Mark.

"That's all!"

"What did you do?"

"We were so scared. We fell flat on our faces. But then we heard Jesus saying very gently, 'Don't be afraid. Get up.'"

Mark was shaking his head. "I don't understand. Every time I think I understand, I hear something new. Then I have to think about it all over again."

"Yeah!" said Peter. "I know what you mean."

FIRST SUNDAY IN LENT

Learning How to Give

BASED ON DEUTERONOMY 26:1–11

The people of Israel didn't have a place to live.

For years and years, they had been wandering around, looking for a place to stay. Then, one day, God led them to a land that looked like a wonderful place to live. "This will be your country," God said. "This will be your new home."

So the people of Israel moved into their new country. They brought their tents and their sheep and their goats and their camels. They brought everything they had.

"What a beautiful country," they said. "There's lots of grass for our animals to eat. There is good ground to grow nice gardens. There are big trees with figs and other fruit we can eat."

"How can we say thank you to God for our new home?" they wondered. "We should say the words, 'thank you' when we pray to God. But we also should *do* something. We should do something that will help us remember how good God as been to us."

Then someone remembered what Moses had said to them. When the people of Israel were wandering around in the desert, Moses, their leader, had told them how to say "thank you" to God. "Whenever you grow something in the ground, or pick something off a tree, give the first part of it to God.

"The first melon from the garden.

"The first fig from the tree.

"The first wine from the grapes.

"The first baby sheep and the first baby goat.

"The first part of everything."

"But how can we give it to God?" they wondered. "God is everywhere. God isn't like a person you can hand something to. When we want to give something to God, what do we do with it?"

They puzzled and puzzled, until someone remembered what else Moses had told them. "Take those first fruits to the place where you worship God."

"That's a good idea," they said. "And then we can use those things to help people who are poor and who don't have enough to eat. That would be a good way to give things to God."

And so from then on whenever the people of Israel gathered the first harvest from their gardens, or picked the first fruits from their trees, they always said, "The first melon goes to God," or "the first of the wine from the grapes goes to God."

Jesus Gets Ready

BASED ON LUKE 4:1–13

"How can I show people how to live God's way?" Jesus wondered.

He prayed to God about this and, deep inside himself, he heard something like a voice without any words. Jesus knew that God wanted him to go into the desert.

But when Jesus got to the lonely desert, it didn't feel as if God was there at all. Jesus felt as if he was all alone. "Maybe God doesn't care about me anymore," Jesus wondered.

Jesus found a lonely place where he could think for a long time. "Maybe if I don't eat any food, and drink just a little water, maybe that will help me know what God wants to me to do."

Jesus prayed many times. "God, please tell me. If I am your Chosen One, what should I do? What should I say to people? What kind of a person should I be?"

Jesus didn't hear God at all. Instead, he began to hear an evil voice inside him. The voice talked about the wrong way to be the Messiah, the Chosen One.

"Look," said the voice inside Jesus. "Here's an easy way to be the Messiah. Turn those stones into bread. You can do it! If you give people lots to eat, they will say you are the Messiah and follow you."

"No," said Jesus. "The scriptures have told us people need more than bread."

"Well then," said the voice. "Go to the top of a mountain. I'll show you all the hills and valleys. I'll show you all the cities and towns. You can be famous. You can be a hero. You can be boss of everyone and everything, if you worship me instead of God. Then everyone will say you are the Messiah."

"No!" said Jesus. "The scriptures have told us to serve only God. Don't serve anyone else."

"Well then," said the voice. "Go to the top of the high temple. Jump off. God will help you. God's angels will set you down gently. You won't hurt yourself. All the people will clap and cheer. Everyone will say you are the Messiah."

"No," said Jesus. "The scriptures have told us. Don't try to test God."

"Bah!" said the voice. "You won this time. But I'll get you later."

Jesus was weak from not having any food. He was tired from all the thinking and praying he had done. "It's going to be really hard to be God's Chosen One," Jesus said to himself.

But he felt strong inside. Jesus knew God had been with him there in the desert. God had helped him choose the right way. Now Jesus was ready to show people how to grow in God's way.

Paul and the Church in Philippi

BASED ON PHILIPPIANS 3:17 – 4:1

Paul was in jail.

He was in jail because the Roman soldiers didn't want him to talk about Jesus. "Paul tells the people that Jesus is more important than the Roman Emperor," said the soldiers. "So he has to go to jail."

Paul wasn't unhappy. He didn't like being in jail. Being in jail was awful. The jail was dark and cold and smelly.

But Paul thought of the many people he had told about Jesus. Paul had travelled to many different places to teach people how to live God's way. And when he thought about them, he felt happy.

One day a visitor came to see Paul. His name was Epaphroditus (ep-a-frow-DI-tus). Epaphroditus came from a city called Philippi and he had a gift for Paul. It was money so that Paul could buy some food and clothes.

"This is from the church at Philippi," said Epaphroditus. "They remember how you came and told them about God's love. They remember the stories about Jesus that you told them. And they are trying very hard to live God's way."

"Thank you for telling me that," said Paul. "When I pray, I know that I am doing God's work, but it's always nice to have people tell me too."

"Then I have some more of God's work for you," said Epaphroditus. "The people in the church at Philippi would like to have a letter from you."

"About what?" asked Paul.

"About what we should do or say. We want to live God's way, but it's hard. Most of the people in Philippi don't believe in God. They don't believe that Jesus was God's Chosen One."

"Well then, let's write a letter," said Paul. "I'll say the words and you write them down."

Epaphroditus went off quickly, and soon he was back with the things to make the letter. "Write this," said Paul.

"To all my friends in Philippi. I say thank you to God every time I think of you. And when I talk to God about you in my prayers, I feel happy.

"My sisters and brothers, look at the people who really try hard to live God's way. People like me, for instance.

"There are some people who live as if they are God's enemies. They only think about the food they eat and about the expensive clothes they wear. You don't need to be like that.

"You are God's people. It is God who will make you feel strong and good, and who will show you how to live in a way that really helps you and other people.

"My brothers and sisters, I love all of you. Sometimes it's hard being God's people, but if you help each other, it will be easier for you.

"Please say 'hello' to all my many friends who are part of God's church in Philippi. And may Jesus the Christ be with you always.

"Your friend,

"Paul."

The Poor People of Jerusalem

BASED ON LUKE 13:31–35

King Herod was afraid.

He didn't look afraid. He looked as if he was really brave. He looked as if nothing ever frightened him.

But deep down inside he was afraid. King Herod was afraid that people would think he wasn't a very good king. Sometimes at night, when he was all alone in his bed, the king would cry.

King Herod was most afraid of people like John the Baptizer. John the Baptizer told everyone about the bad things the king had done. And so the king told his soldiers to put John the Baptizer in jail.

King Herod didn't like Jesus either. Jesus told people how much God loved them. He told them how to live God's way. "They should do what I tell them to do," said the king. "Not what God tells them to do."

Jesus was not afraid of King Herod. "The king takes food and money away from poor people," Jesus said. "The king should help poor people. He shouldn't take away their food and clothes."

When Jesus went to the big city of Jerusalem, some of his friends were worried. "Go way from here," they said to Jesus. "King Herod wants to kill you!"

"I have a message for that fox," said Jesus. His friends could tell Jesus was angry because his eyes were sparkling. "You tell King Herod that I am helping sick people get better. I am helping people who are in trouble. And these people here in Jerusalem need a lot of help."

Then Jesus looked around at all the people gathered in Jerusalem. His eyes didn't look angry anymore. Now they looked sad. Jesus could see that so many of them didn't have enough to eat. They didn't have enough clothes. He could see that they were all afraid of King Herod, who wanted everything for himself.

"Oh, Jerusalem! Jerusalem!" said Jesus. "You are afraid of King Herod, and so you are afraid of the people he hates. When God sends prophets to help you, you throw stones at them. You tell them to go away, just the way you told me to go away."

There were tears in Jesus' eyes as he looked at the people in the city. "How often I've wanted to gather you all together," he said. "I wanted to hold you close and protect you – the way a mother hen takes care of her baby chicks – the way she gathers them under her wings and keeps them warm and safe. But you wouldn't let me do that."

Jesus felt very sad. He knew he could help the people of Jerusalem, but only if they wanted him to help. Only if they listened to his stories about God's love.

THIRD SUNDAY IN LENT

You Can't Buy Love

BASED ON ISAIAH 55:1–9

Rebekah was Old Isaiah's best friend. She went to visit him every day and he was always glad to see her.

One day Rebekah and her friends were building houses and roads in the sand. Along came Asher waving a big wooden sword. "Look what my dad gave me," yelled Asher. "Get out of my way or I'll cut you with my sword!"

Asher knocked over the house Rebekah had been building in the sand.

"Stop that!" Rebekah said. "You just wrecked my nice house!"

But Asher kept swinging his sword. He swung it right close to Rebekah and she put up her arm to protect her face. The sword hit her arm. It hurt!

"You are mean and awful!" yelled Rebekah. She and her friends got up and went away. They left Asher all by himself swinging his sword.

The next morning Rebekah went to visit Old Isaiah. She showed him the blue spot on her arm where Asher's sword hit her.

"Why did Asher do that?" Old Isaiah asked.

"He's always doing things like that," said Rebekah. "We don't like to play with him because he always tries to pretend he's so big and strong and tough."

"Why does Asher do that?" Old Isaiah asked again.

"When we build houses and roads in the sand, Asher doesn't build very nice houses, and so he wrecks his own house and everybody else's too."

"Why does Asher do that?"

"Why do you keep asking me the same question over and over?"

"Because you can't make things better until you answer the hard questions."

"Then ask Asher," said Rebekah. "He's the one who keeps doing mean things."

"No, I'm asking you." Old Isaiah almost sounded a little angry.

"I guess he wants us to pay attention to him. He wants us to play with him. But we don't, because he's too mean."

"Rebekah," said Old Isaiah, "In the marketplace where I go every morning, I see people like Asher. They buy really nice clothes because they think that will make people like them. They buy bright shiny tools and swords and knives because it makes them feel important. They buy many kinds of delicious food because when they are eating they feel good."

"That doesn't help," said Rebekah. "They're just like Asher. People won't like you because you have nice clothes or shiny tools."

"And people feel good while they are eating food or drinking wine, but as soon as they stop they feel unhappy again. It's very sad," said Old Isaiah.

"Why do they do that?" Rebekah smiled because now she was asking Old Isaiah's hard question.

"We all need other people. We all need to be loved. I need you to love me, Rebekah, and you need me to love you. And we all need God."

"But hitting people with swords or buying nice clothes doesn't make anyone love you," said Rebekah. "It doesn't even make anyone *like* you. It sure doesn't make God love you."

Rebekah and Old Isaiah were quiet for a while. Then, almost in a whisper, Rebekah said, "I'm going to invite Asher to come and play with me at my house. I like Asher when he isn't pretending to be big and tough. Maybe we can learn to play together and he'll know that I am his friend."

"And I've got a song," said Old Isaiah. "I'm going to give my song to the people in the marketplace – the people who are always buying clothes and tools and food to make themselves feel good."

"Are you going to put that song in your book?" asked Rebekah.

Old Isaiah smiled at Rebekah, and began to sing his song.

Ho! Are you thirsty?
Ho! Are you hungry?

Here's nice cold water.
You don't need money.
Here's good, rich food.
It's free.

Don't spend your money
buying things that don't help.
The things you buy,
won't make friends love you.
The things you buy,
won't gain God's love.

God has promised you!
God loves you as you are!
You can't buy things that make God love you!
You can't buy things that make friends care.

Live God's way!
Be kind and good and fair!
Love yourself, the way God made you,
then God and friends will love you too.

THIRD SUNDAY IN LENT

God Doesn't Do Things Like That

BASED ON LUKE 13:1–9

People liked to hear Jesus talk.

Sometimes many people gathered – so many that Jesus had to talk very loudly so that everyone could hear.

Sometimes the people asked Jesus questions. Often they were very hard questions.

One day when Jesus had been telling many stories about God's love, a woman in the crowd shouted, "Jesus, I have a question for you."

"Tell me your question," Jesus said.

"Do you remember when the people from Galilee came into the Temple to pray, and the soldiers rushed in and killed them all?"

"Yes, I remember that," said Jesus. "It was terrible."

"Well, tell me, Jesus," said the woman. "Did God let them be killed because they had done some really bad things?"

"No," said Jesus. "God doesn't do things like that. They were killed because Pilate, the governor, was angry at them. He sent his soldiers to kill them."

"Well, what about those 18 people in Siloam?" This time it was a man in the crowd who was asking the question. "They all died when the tower they were building fell on them. Did God make that happen because they had done bad things?"

"No," said Jesus. "God doesn't do things like that. The tower wasn't built right. It was weak. That's why it fell on those men."

Jesus looked around at the people. But they didn't seem to have any more questions.

"God doesn't hurt people because they have done bad things," Jesus said. "God wants you to be sorry for any bad things you have done. God wants you try hard to live a better way. God wants you to be happy and wants good things to happen in your life."

Some of the people in the crowd looked puzzled. "Let me tell you a story." Jesus could see the people smiling. They liked his stories.

"This is a very short story," said Jesus. "It's about a farmer who had a fig tree. The farmer asked a friend what she should do about the fig tree. 'It was a very nice tree but it doesn't give me any figs.'

"'I know what to do,' said her friend. 'Dig around the tree. Loosen up the earth so the water can get down to the roots. Put a little fertilizer around the tree. That will help it grow stronger.'

"God is like the farmer's friend," said Jesus. "God is always trying to help you grow and be strong, so that good things will happen in your life."

FOURTH SUNDAY IN LENT

I'm Happy Again

BASED ON PSALM 32

I'm happy again. Yes, I am.
I'm happy because I told God.
I told God about
the wrong things I did,
and I said to God, "I am sorry."

For a long, long time I felt bad.
I was always worried and sad.
I didn't tell God about wrong things I did.
I didn't tell God anything.

But now I'm happy again.
I can sing! I can dance! I can play!
I told God about the wrong things I did,
and I said to God, "I am sorry."

I said to God, "I'm sorry,
I'll try now to live in your way.
I'll try to be kind to the person I hurt,
I'll try to be friends once again."
I'm happy again. Yes, I am.
I'm happy because I told God.
I told God about
the wrong things I did,
and I said to God, "I am sorry."

A Loving Father

BASED ON LUKE 15:1–3a, 11–32

Not everyone liked Jesus. Sometimes people got very angry at him. They didn't like the things he did and said.

"Jesus shouldn't be friends with those people," they said. "We're the important ones. We're the best. Jesus should only be friends with people like us!"

"God loves everyone," said Jesus. "Even people who sometimes do bad things. Listen. I'll tell you a story about how God loves us, even when we are not being good."

Jesus was a very good storyteller. So everyone was ready to listen.

"My story is about a father who had two sons," said Jesus. "The younger son said to his father, 'I hate it around here. If you were dead, then half of your money would be mine.'

"That made the father very sad. But instead of getting angry, he said, 'You can have half of my money. Right now. Here it is.'

"So the younger son took the money and left. He went far away from his home. The son spent his money on wild parties and expensive food. He never wrote a letter home to say 'thank you.' After a while, his father wondered if his son had died.

"But soon the money was all gone. The son felt very hungry, but now he had no food and no money either. So he got a job looking after someone's pigs.

"'This is awful,' he thought. 'Here I am looking after these stinky pigs. I hate pigs. I wish I could go back home.'

"The son knew he had made his father very sad. 'My dad would never let me come back home after what I did. Except maybe, if I say I'm sorry. Maybe if I just ask to be a helper, a servant, he might let me come back home.'

"So the son started walking back home. He was still a long way off when he saw his father running down the road toward him.

"'Father, I'm so sorry…' But his father wouldn't let him finish. Instead, his father threw his arms around him and gave him a kiss.

"Then the father called to everyone. 'Come to our house. We're having a big party tonight. My son has come home! My son has come home! Let's have a party! Let's celebrate!'

"They had the biggest party you ever saw. But the father noticed that his older son wasn't with them. So the father went looking for him.

"The father found the older son sitting all by himself out in the backyard. 'Why aren't you at our party?' the father asked.

"'It's not fair,' said the older brother. 'I stayed at home. I was a faithful son. I did all the things you asked. That other son of yours ran away and spent all the money you gave him. Then when he came home you had a big party. You never had a party for me!'

"'My son,' said the father, 'I've been able to show my love for you every day. Your brother was lost. Now he's found. I felt as if your brother was dead. Now he's alive. Let's be glad. Your brother is part of our family again!'"

FIFTH SUNDAY IN LENT

A Song of Happiness

BASED ON PSALM 126

When God made us happy again,
it was as if we awoke from a dream.
Then we laughed and we sang,
we shouted for joy,
because God was so good to us!

We were sad and our lives were so hard,
but we planted our seeds and we prayed.
Then God blessed the seeds and they grew.
So we laughed and we sang,
we shouted for joy,
because God was so good to us!

May all hurting people learn how to laugh,
when they find they don't hurt anymore.
May the ones who are hungry shout for joy,
when they find good food to eat.

Something Beautiful for Jesus

BASED ON JOHN 12:1–8

One day Jesus went to visit his friends who lived in the town of Bethany. His friends were named Lazarus, Mary, and Martha. They were brother and sisters.

Lazarus was the one who had died, but Jesus brought him back to life again.

When Jesus came to visit them, Mary, Martha, and Lazarus said, "Let's make a nice dinner for Jesus and his friends." So they prepared some good food.

While they were eating, Mary brought some perfume. It smelled beautiful, and Mary had to pay a lot of money to buy it. She poured the perfume on Jesus' feet. That was her way of showing Jesus that she loved him.

Judas, one of Jesus' friends, didn't like what Mary did. "We could have sold that perfume for a lot of money. Then we could have used that money to buy food for people who have nothing to eat!"

"Leave her alone," said Jesus. "Mary has done a beautiful thing. She knows that soon I will have to go to Jerusalem and that I will probably be killed there. So she is getting my body ready to be buried."

"But what about the poor people?" asked Judas.

"You will always have poor people to help. But you won't always have me here."

Judas shook his head. He didn't understand what Jesus meant.

Neither did Mary.

But she was glad she had poured the perfume on Jesus' feet.

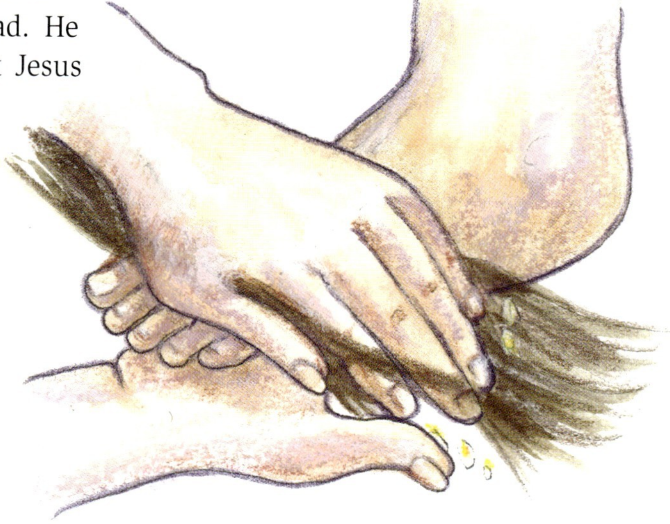

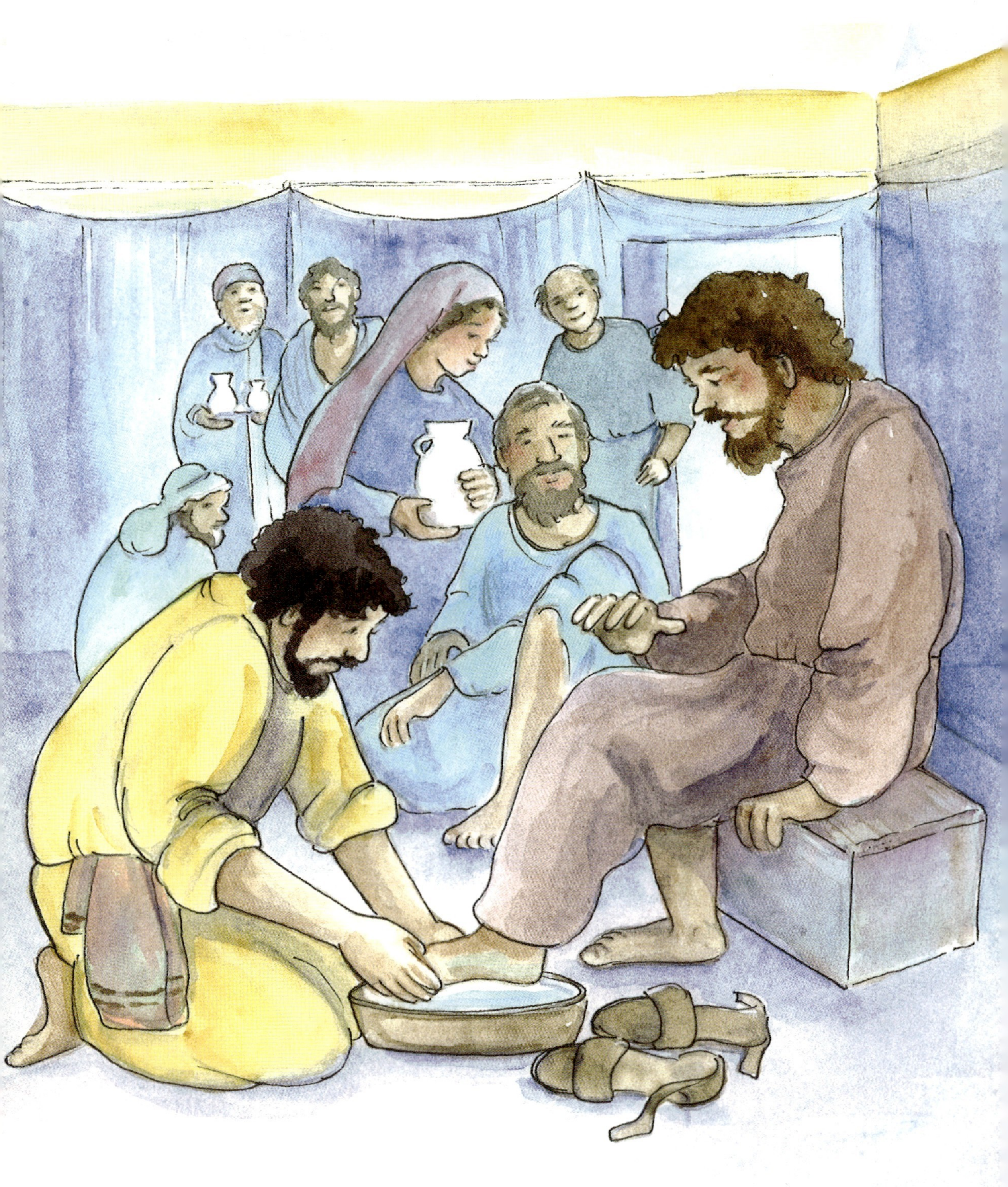

Washing Feet

BASED ON JOHN 13:1–20

"What are you doing?" Peter asked. Jesus had poured some water into a basin. Then Jesus tied a towel around his waist.

"I'm going to wash your feet," said Jesus.

"What?" said Peter. "You shouldn't do that. Let me call a servant. It's a servant's job to wash feet."

Jesus and the disciples lived in a hot, dry country. The roads were very dusty. A few rich people rode along the road on horses. A few people got to ride on donkeys. But most people walked when they needed to go somewhere. Their feet got hot and tired and dirty.

When people came to visit, they liked to have their feet washed. It made them feel clean and rested. Rich people had servants who washed feet. Important people didn't wash other people's feet.

That's why Peter thought it was awful when Jesus said, "I'm going to wash your feet."

"No," said Peter. "You will never wash my feet."

"Peter," said Jesus, "God wants me to be your servant. When I am your servant, and you are my servant, then we can really be friends."

"I want to be friends more than anything," said Peter. "You can wash me all over if it will help us be friends."

"Just your feet," smiled Jesus. So Jesus washed Peter's feet. Then he washed the other disciples' feet too.

When he finished, Jesus told his friends why he had done this.

"Sometimes you call me 'Teacher' and sometimes you call me 'Lord.' That's fine. That's what I am. But when I washed your feet, I showed you that I am also your servant.

"You should wash each other's feet too. You should be servants to each other. I have shown you how to live in God's way. Be each other's servants."

Jesus the Servant

BASED ON LUKE 22:7–13, 24–29

Jesus and the disciples had come to Jerusalem for a very special reason. They wanted to celebrate the Passover there.

Jewish people celebrate Passover to remember the time God helped them escape from being slaves in Egypt.

Jesus said to his friends Peter and John, "Go find a place where we can eat together. Get the food ready, so we can have our Passover meal."

Peter and John were happy to do this. "Where should we go to make dinner?"

"Here's what you do," said Jesus. "Go into the city and look for a man carrying a jar of water. Follow him. When he leads you into a house, say to the person who owns the house, 'The teacher would like to know where he can have the Passover meal with his friends.' The owner of the house will show you a big room upstairs. It will have tables and everything else we need. Get that room ready for us."

Near the end of the day, Jesus and the disciples got together in the room that Peter and John had found. All the food was ready.

Jesus wanted the disciples to know this would be a very special Passover. "Some important things are going to happen soon," he said. "This may be the last time I eat with you."

The disciples weren't really listening. They were arguing.

"I'm better than you are!" one of them said.

"You are not!"

"I am so!"

"My friends, please!" said Jesus. "That's how people argue when they don't know about living God's way. But that's not the way you should act.

"When we live God's way, things are different. The one who is weakest is more important than the one who is strongest. The one who is poorest is loved more than the one who is rich.

"I am your servant. I have come to help you and to help others. That's what a servant does. I'm not here to be your boss. I don't want to be your ruler. I want to be your friend."

The disciples tried hard to understand. But it didn't make sense. "Jesus is the Messiah, God's Chosen One," they said. "How can the boss be a servant?"

Jesus Prays in the Garden

BASED ON LUKE 22:39–46

When Jesus and the disciples had finished their Passover meal, Jesus wanted to find a quiet place to pray. He went to the Mount of Olives, and the disciples followed him. The night was very dark. All of them were worried and afraid, so they sang quietly as they walked.

They came to a quiet garden. "Please sit here under the trees," Jesus said to the disciples. "I want to go over there and pray. While I'm praying, you do some praying too. There will be some scary times soon and you need to ask God to make you strong."

The disciples had never seen Jesus look so worried and afraid. They watched him walk away, not very far, about as far as you could throw a stone. They huddled together and listened as Jesus started to pray.

"Oh God!" said Jesus in a loud voice. Then he fell, face down, on the ground. He was almost shouting. "My Father, oh my Father, does this have to happen? Isn't there any way I can get out of this?"

Jesus prayed to God for a long time. He didn't say many words. Mostly he seemed to be listening. Finally, almost in a whisper, he said, "Not what I want, God, but what you want. I will do what you want me to do."

When Jesus finished praying, he looked over at the disciples. They were asleep. Jesus woke them. "Couldn't you just stay awake with me for a little while?" he said sadly. "Never mind. I understand. In your minds you want to stay awake, but your bodies are too tired."

God's Chosen One

BASED ON LUKE 23:33–43

Mary Magdalene and Susanna couldn't even cry anymore. They had no tears left to cry.

But they couldn't go home. They had to stay with Jesus while he was dying on the cross. They loved him so much. "We can't let him die alone," they said.

Both of the women felt numb, as if they didn't have any feeling left in their bodies – as if even their brains had gone to sleep.

Then they heard some talking. "How can they talk?" asked Mary. She looked up at where Jesus was hanging on the cross – all bloody and horrible, like the two other men, one hanging on each side of him.

Mary noticed the soldiers who were supposed to be guarding Jesus, to make sure nobody tried to save him. The soldiers were asleep now. Mary remembered how one of the soldiers had yelled up at Jesus on the cross. "They say you're God's Chosen One. So why don't you just jump down off that cross?" The soldier laughed. Jesus didn't say anything.

The voice Mary heard came from one of the men hanging on crosses beside Jesus. "So are you God's Chosen One?" he asked Jesus. "Why don't you save yourself and save us at the same time." He tried to laugh, but it hurt too much.

Then the man on the other side of Jesus spoke. "You shouldn't talk like that. You and I are here because of bad things we did. We stole things and killed people. Jesus didn't do anything bad."

Then he looked at Jesus. "Jesus," he said, "please remember me when you go to be with God."

"My friend…" Jesus could hardly talk. His voice was just a whisper. "Today, you and I will be together when we go to live with God."

Mary and Susanna put their arms around each other. They had cried so much they didn't think they had any tears left, but they cried some more anyway. "Jesus was kind and gentle to that man," said Susanna. "Even though he was hurting terribly and dying, Jesus was kind and gentle."

"He really is God's Chosen One," said Mary.

EASTER SUNDAY

Jesus Is Alive!

BASED ON LUKE 24:1–12

Note to leaders and parents: *The story of the encounter between Mary of Magdala and the risen Christ (John 20:1–18) is suggested for all three Easter Sundays in the lectionary cycle, probably because it is such a beautiful and moving story. It can be found on page 98 of the* Lectionary Story Bible, Year A.

Joanna felt very, very sad. So sad she could hardly walk. She didn't cry, but her eyes felt dry and sore, as if they needed to cry. But the tears wouldn't come.

Joanna tried to sleep. But all she could do was think of how she had watched Jesus die on the cross. She and Mary of Magdala and some of the other women had helped take Jesus' dead body down from the cross. They had carried it to a small cave.

Joanna remembered how they gently laid Jesus' body down. Some helpers rolled a big stone in front of the opening to the cave. Then the two women went home. Joanna thought about this over and over as she tried to sleep.

The next day, Joanna just sat around. It was the Sabbath, and usually on the Sabbath Jewish people have a nice meal and they sit around and talk. But Joanna and Mary of Magdala and the other women didn't want to eat. They didn't feel like talking. They didn't feel like anything.

The next day Mary said, "When people die, their families often take spices and oils and things that smell nice, and put it on the dead person's body. I think we are Jesus' family. Don't you think so, Joanna?"

Joanna nodded. "Of course. Let's do it."

So Mary and Joanna gathered up the spices and the sweet smelling ointments. Very early in the morning, they went to the place where they had put Jesus' body.

"What?" Joanna stopped walking. "Look, Mary! The stone has been rolled away!"

"Who would do that?" asked Mary.

Joanna started running as fast as she could. She looked inside the cave. "Mary!" she yelled. "Jesus' body is gone! Who could have done this?"

Joanna and Mary didn't know what to do. They just stood in front of the cave looking at each other. They were afraid and all mixed up.

Suddenly, two people were standing there – two people in shining white clothes. Mary and Joanna were very afraid. "Are you an angel?" Joanna whispered.

"This is a place for those who are dead," said one of the people. "But you are looking for Jesus who is alive! He isn't dead anymore."

Mary looked at Joanna and Joanna looked at Mary. They didn't know what to say or do or think. "But…but…I don't…?" Joanna tried to say something, but the words got all mixed up.

"Don't you remember?" asked the other person in shining clothes. "Jesus told you this while he was still near your home in Galilee. He told you that he was going to be arrested by the people who hated him and that they would kill him. But he also said that he would come alive again. Don't you remember?"

Joanna looked at Mary again and Mary looked at Joanna. They turned back to say something to the two people in shining clothes, but they were gone. They had disappeared. And the two women stood there. They didn't know what to think or what to do.

Finally Joanna spoke. "Let's go tell the others."

Without waiting for Mary to answer, she began running and Mary ran after her. They found their friends – the people who had been with Jesus – sitting around looking sad.

"We have wonderful news!" they yelled. Both Mary and Joanna started talking at the same time, telling them what had happened, about the people in shining clothes, about the stone being rolled away, and about how Jesus was alive again.

But the friends of Jesus just sat there. The men didn't believe Mary and Joanna. "But it's true! It's true!" Joanna was laughing and crying at the same time. "It's true. Jesus is alive again!"

Peter got up slowly. His eyes looked red and tired. He looked at Mary and Joanna for a long time. "I'll go and see," he said. His voice was quiet and scratchy from crying.

They all sat there, waiting for Peter to come back. It seemed like forever. Joanna and Mary were still smiling, but everybody else looked glum and tired. "Maybe it was just a dream," Mary whispered to Joanna.

Then the door opened. It was Peter. His eyes were shining and he was all out of breath from running.

"It's true!" Peter was trying to shout, but his voice was too scratchy. "It's true! It's true! It's true!"

Make Happy Sounds for God

BASED ON PSALM 150

Note to leaders and parents: *The story of Thomas, John 20:24–29, appears in the* Lectionary Story Bible, Years A and B, *on pages 100 and 102 respectively.*

Make happy sounds for God!
Make happy sounds for God in church.
Make happy sounds for God who is everywhere.
Make happy sounds for God who has done great things.

Make happy sounds with a trumpet.
Make happy sounds with a harp.
Make happy sounds with drums and bells.
Make happy movements with your body.
Dance for God!

Make happy sounds for God,
with fiddles and flutes.
Make happy sounds for God,
with loud crashing cymbals.

Let everything that can move
and breathe,
make happy sounds for God!

If That's What God Wants

BASED ON ACTS 5:17–42

After Jesus died and rose again, the friends of Jesus – the disciples – gathered together to remember what Jesus said and did.

They went all over the city of Jerusalem telling people about Jesus. That made the religious leaders angry. It made them *so* angry that they grabbed some of the disciples and threw them into jail.

But then a strange thing happened. In the middle of the night, when it was very, very dark, the door of the prison opened up. Just like that!

"It must be an angel," said Andrew as they walked out.

And then they heard something that sounded like a loud whisper. "Go to the Temple and tell all the people there about Jesus."

So before the sun came up in the morning, Andrew and Peter and the other disciples were at the Temple. "We want to tell you about Jesus, and about God's love," they said.

Then the leaders got *really* angry. "Go and bring those friends of Jesus over here," they said to the soldiers.

So Peter and Andrew and the others were brought to the leaders. "Why are you doing this?" the leaders asked. "We told you, when we put you in jail, that we didn't want you telling people stories about Jesus."

"Yes, we know you told us that," said Peter. "But we have to do what God tells us. And God wants us to tell stories about Jesus. God wants us to tell people that Jesus was killed, but that he became alive again. God wants us all to know about God's love."

That made the leaders furious. "We should kill them!" they said.

Then one of the leaders, Gamaliel, stood up. "Be careful," Gamaliel said. "If it's true what they say – that God wants them to tell people about this Jesus – then there is nothing you can do to stop them. If it's not true, if that is *not* what God wants, then it won't be long before people get tired of their talking and everyone will forget about Jesus."

"Yes," said the other leaders. "That makes sense." So they told the soldiers to give Peter and Andrew and the other disciples a good beating. "Tell them to stop talking about Jesus, and then let them go."

The disciples were badly hurt by the beatings. But as soon as they could, they went out again and told more and more people about Jesus.

And each day, more and more people said, "Yes, I think Jesus was God's Chosen One. I would like to be a friend of Jesus. I would like to be part of his church."

THIRD SUNDAY OF EASTER

Saul Learns about Jesus

BASED ON ACTS 9:1–19, 22:3–16, 26:4–18

Saul hated Christians. "They are saying that Jesus was God's Chosen One. That isn't true!"

So Saul went to the leaders and said, "Let me get those Christians, the ones they call People of the Way. Let me throw them into jail so they don't tell any more lies about Jesus."

The leaders gave Saul a letter. "Saul can put all the Christians in jail," the letter said.

"I'm going to Damascus," said Saul. "There are many Christians in Damascus. I want to throw them into jail. I want them to stop talking about Jesus."

On the way to Damascus, a strange thing happened to Saul. Suddenly, he saw a very bright light. It was so bright Saul couldn't see anymore. Then Saul heard someone speaking to him.

"Saul, Saul," said the voice. "Why are you hurting me?"

"Who is this?" Saul asked. He was very afraid.

"I am Jesus, the one you are hurting," said the voice. "Now get up and go into Damascus. I'll tell you what to do later."

When Saul got up from the ground, he was blind. He couldn't see anything. The people who were with Saul helped him walk. They got him into Damascus. But Saul didn't know what to do. He couldn't eat. He couldn't see. He was afraid.

Ananias lived in Damascus. Ananias tried hard to live in God's way.

One day, Ananias knew that God was telling him something. "Go and find the man named Saul. He needs your help."

"But Saul is trying to capture us," said Ananias. "He wants to put Christians in jail."

"Go," God said to Ananias. "Saul has changed. Saul has learned about Jesus."

So Ananias went and found Saul. Ananias put his hands on Saul's head and said, "My brother, Saul. The spirit of Jesus has come into your heart."

Then Saul opened his eyes. "I can see again!" he shouted. "I can see!"

Saul stood up and walked around the room. He was very excited. "I need to know all about Jesus," he said to Ananias. "You have to tell me everything. Everything!"

Ananias smiled. "I'll tell you everything I know, Saul. But I think you need something to eat and drink first. You haven't had anything for days."

"Then talk while I'm eating," said Saul. "Tell me more about Jesus."

Ananias told Saul many of the stories that Jesus told. He talked about how Jesus had been killed by the soldiers, and how he was alive again.

"Ananias," said Saul. "Now I believe that Jesus really is God's Chosen One. I would like to become one of the People of the Way. I would like to be baptized."

And so it was that Saul, who had tried to hurt the People of the Way, became one of them. Soon he began telling other people about Jesus. He went to many different places and talked to many people. He told them that Jesus was really God's Chosen One. And he wrote many letters, which are in our Bible.

Saul was Jewish. He told many people who were not Jews about living in God's way. People who are not Jewish call Saul by a different name. They call him Paul.

THIRD SUNDAY OF EASTER

Peter Learns

BASED ON JOHN 21:1–17

It was several weeks after Jesus had been killed. The disciples got together often to talk about Jesus and to remember the things he had said and done.

"I wonder what Jesus wants us to do now?" Peter often asked the other disciples. "He lived with us here. He taught us many things about God and about each other. Then Jesus was killed, but we know he's alive again. So what do we do now?

"We might as well go fishing," Peter said. He and some of the other disciples got into their boat and rowed out into the lake. They fished and fished, all night long. They were all very tired.

"We haven't caught a thing," said Peter. "We might as well row back to the shore."

As they got closer to the edge of the lake, Peter heard a voice calling from the shore. It was still quite dark. Peter couldn't see who it was.

"My friends," called the voice. "Have you caught any fish?"

"No. None at all!" Peter called back.

"Put your net on the other side of the boat," the voice called. "You'll find some fish there."

So that's what they did. In no time at all, the net was so full of fish they thought it would break.

"I know who that is," said one of the disciples. "That's Jesus. Who else knows where the fish are?"

Peter got very excited. He jumped into the water and swam to shore. The other disciples rowed the boat up to the beach. It was hard, because it was so heavy with many fish. "There were 153 fish in that net," said Thomas.

"Bring some of the fish here," said Jesus. "We'll cook them for breakfast." Jesus had built a little fire on the shore.

"Mmmm, these taste good," said Peter. Jesus laughed. He looked at Peter, whose mouth was full of fish. Then, suddenly, Jesus looked a little sad.

"Peter," said Jesus. "Do you love me?"

"Sure," said Peter. "You know that."

"Then feed my lambs," said Jesus.

Jesus didn't say anything for a while. Peter kept on eating fish, but he wondered what Jesus meant. They had a lot of fish, but there weren't any sheep in sight.

"Peter," said Jesus. "Do you really love me?"

"Of course, Jesus," said Peter. "You know I love you."

"Take care of my sheep," said Jesus.

Jesus was quiet again. Peter had stopped eating. He was thinking hard about what Jesus had said. What did Jesus mean – "Feed my sheep"?

After a while, Jesus spoke again. He spoke so quietly, Peter could hardly hear.

"Peter, do you love me?"

Peter felt hurt. Why did Jesus keep asking him the same question? "You know everything, Jesus," he said. "You know that I love you."

"Feed my sheep."

That was the last time that Peter and the other disciples saw Jesus. But they knew he was alive.

Jesus was alive in their hearts. The disciples felt Jesus was somehow with them whenever they talked about him. When they prayed, they knew Jesus was listening to their prayers.

And many, many times, Peter thought about that last time with Jesus. And he could hear Jesus saying to him, "Feed my sheep." Now Peter knew what Jesus meant.

Peter knew that when Jesus said, "Feed my sheep," Jesus wanted Peter to help people, God's sheep, to live in God's way.

Dorcas and Anna Help Each Other

BASED ON ACTS 9:36–42

There is a very short story in the Bible about a person named Dorcas. The Bible only tells us a small part of her story. It says she was a very kind woman who helped many people. So I read what the Bible said about Dorcas and then made up the rest of the story myself.

Why not read about Dorcas in your Bible? You might want to make up your own story about her.

"Here," said Dorcas. "Put this on. It will keep you warm at night."

"Oh, thank you," said Anna. "Thank you very much."

Anna was eight years old. She was all by herself. She had no mother and no father and no place to live. She had to sleep outside on the street at night.

Dorcas smiled at Anna. "Here's something to eat. You look hungry."

Anna gobbled up the food. She was very hungry. Anna hadn't eaten for three whole days. She was also very lonely and afraid.

After Anna had eaten the food, she felt a little better. Dorcas sat down beside her. "Do you have a place to live? Is there anyone to take care of you?"

Anna shook her head.

"Well then," said Dorcas. "Would it be all right if I found you a place to live?"

"Yes, please," said Anna in a tiny voice.

"Would you stay with me until we can find you a home?" Dorcas asked. Anna nodded.

Dorcas took Anna's hand as they walked. It seemed a long way.

Then Dorcas began to walk more slowly. She wasn't feeling very well. "No matter," said Dorcas to herself. "I'll be fine soon. I've got to find Anna a place to live."

Dorcas could hardly walk by the time she and Anna got to the house. "Anna," said Dorcas, "would you mind if I just lie down for a while? I'm very tired. All I need is a little rest and then I'll be fine."

But Dorcas wasn't fine. She lay down and closed her eyes. She was very, very still. Anna looked closely. She couldn't see Dorcas breathing. Anna was very worried about her new friend.

Anna ran to the door. She saw one of the neighbours outside. "Please," she said. "Please come quickly. Something is wrong."

"Oh, no," said the neighbour when she came inside. "Dorcas is dead!" The neighbour began to cry very loudly.

Soon other friends heard the crying and came to look. "What will we do?" they cried. "Dorcas was such a good friend. Dorcas always showed us how to live in God's way. Look at the coat she made for me when I was cold."

"She was the only friend I ever had," thought Anna. "Oh God, please don't let her die."

Many people came to see Dorcas. They remembered how often she had helped poor people. She helped them with food and often made clothes for them. Dorcas loved and helped anyone who needed her.

Someone had called Peter. "Look at Dorcas," they said to Peter. "We think she's dead."

"Please, would you all leave the room for a while," said Peter. "I'd like to be alone with Dorcas."

Everyone went into the next room. Anna too.

Peter prayed very quietly to God. Peter thanked God for Dorcas. "She showed so many people how to live in God's way," said Peter. "Dorcas helped so many people."

Then Peter looked at Dorcas. "We need you, Dorcas. Please get up."

Slowly, Dorcas opened her eyes. She looked at Peter. Peter took her by the hand and helped her out of bed. They walked into the next room where all the people were waiting.

"Look!" the neighbour shouted. "Dorcas is alive!"

"Oh, what's all the fuss," Dorcas said, pretending to be angry. "Go home, all of you. Come, Anna. We've got work to do."

When the people were gone, Dorcas looked at Anna. "Please sit with me for a little while, Anna. Hold my hand. I feel better. But I need someone to be gentle and kind to me right now, while I rest. Would you do that, Anna?"

Anna snuggled up to Dorcas and closed her eyes. Deep in her heart, Anna said, "Thank you, God."

Sing a Song for God

BASED ON PSALM 148

Sing a song for God!
Let everything in the sky
sing for God!
Let all the angels
sing for God!
Let the sun, the moon, the stars,
all sing for God!

Mountains and hills and fruit trees,
all sing for God!
Let all the animals
sing for God!

Kings and queens and everyone
all sing for God!
All the men and women
all the children,
all the old and all
the young,
let all the people
sing for God!

Let everyone
sing for God!

FIFTH SUNDAY OF EASTER

John's Beautiful Dream

BASED ON REVELATION 21:1–6

Note to leaders and parents: *A story based on Acts 11:1–18, which is one of the readings for this Sunday, may be found in the* Lectionary Story Bible, Year A, *page 44.*

There was a time when it was very dangerous to be a friend of Jesus. Christians were often hurt or thrown into jail or killed. The Emperor wanted people to pray to him, as if he were God. Christians didn't want to do that. Jesus had told the Christians about God. They knew the Emperor wasn't God.

Almost 100 years after Jesus had been born on the earth, a man by the name of John was sent to a lonely island called Patmos. John was taken to this island because he was a Christian. He wasn't allowed to go home.

While John was a prisoner on this island, he wrote a very long letter to his Christian friends. It is the last book of our Bible, and it is called Revelation.

John wanted to help his friends be brave. He knew how hard it was to be a Christian. John wanted his friends to know that even though some people hated them, and even though they were often hurt or killed because they were Christian, God had not forgotten them. God loved them. God was still with them and a better time was coming when they could worship God without being afraid.

In the book of Revelation, John tells about some strange dreams he had. They seem kind of mixed up and weird to us now, but John's friends knew what they meant. God was helping them through John's strange dreams.

From John
To the seven churches of Asia,

I have had a most wonderful dream. I want to tell you about it. I hope my dream will help you feel strong, even though the soldiers may come and hurt you, or take you away and even kill you.

But I know that God still loves you. And God has some wonderful plans for you. This is what I saw in my dream.

I saw a new heaven. And a new earth.

The old earth was gone. All the bad things went away.

And then I saw a city. It was Jerusalem – the same Jerusalem where they killed Jesus. Now it was all new and wonderful.

Jerusalem was like a bride in a beautiful dress – all bright and shining.

And then I heard a voice. It was a strong voice.

"God has come to be with the people.
God will live with us, and we will be God's people.
God will wipe away the tears from our eyes.
People won't be killed anymore.
They won't cry because they are hurt.
All the things that were bad and hurtful are gone."

Then, in my dream, I saw God sitting on a throne. And God said, "Look. I am making everything new and beautiful."

Then God told me to write these words. I know they are true because they came from God.

"I am the beginning and the end. I am God, and I am everything. To those who are thirsty and weak, I will give my special water – water that will make them feel strong and whole."

That was my beautiful dream. It made me feel better. I hope it makes you feel better too.

SIXTH SUNDAY OF EASTER

Lydia Starts a New Church

BASED ON ACTS 16:11–15

Do you remember the stories of a man named Paul? If you don't, you could read the story of how he learned about Jesus. It is on page 122 of this book.

Paul travelled to many places to tell people the stories about Jesus. Here's a story about how Paul helped a woman named Lydia to start a church.

"Look," said Lydia to her friend Prisca. Those two men walking toward us by the river. Are they Jews?"

"I hope so," said Prisca. "There are so few of us here in Philippi. We don't even have enough people for a synagogue. We have to come down here to the river when we want to pray."

"Hello!" said Lydia to the two men. "Welcome to Philippi. My name is Lydia. This is Prisca."

"My name is Paul," said one of the men. "And this is my friend Silas. We are looking for the Jewish people who come to the river to pray."

"I wasn't born Jewish," said Lydia. "But I worship the same God. And my friends and I have come here to pray. As you can see, we are five women. A very small group. We would be pleased if you would join us for prayer."

They sang a song first. Then they prayed. They remembered the words of some of the prophets. Soon they were talking about the stories of Abraham and Sarah, about the prophets, and about God's promises.

It wasn't long before Paul and Silas told Lydia and her friends about Jesus. Paul could see that Lydia was really glad to hear about Jesus.

"That is good news," Lydia said to Paul. "Jesus came to show us what God is like and how to live in God's way. God's love is for everybody. That is *really* good news."

Paul and Lydia talked some more. Then Lydia said, "Paul, could I be baptized? I feel the Spirit of Jesus in me. I would like to be Jesus' friend. I want to learn how to live God's way."

So Paul and Lydia went into the river. Paul dipped Lydia under the water for a moment and said a short prayer to God. Then he lifted her out of the water.

"I feel all clean inside," said Lydia.

By this time, it was getting late. Everyone was feeling hungry.

"Would you come to my house for supper?" Lydia asked.

"Thank you," said Paul. "But we can buy our own food. It would cost too much for you to feed us."

"Don't worry," said Lydia. "I sell purple cloth to rich people. It's a good business. I have enough money. Please come and stay with me."

So Paul and Silas stayed with Lydia the whole time they were in Philippi. They went around the city and talked about Jesus.

Some of the things they said made people angry. Paul and Silas were thrown into jail. Lydia wondered if the leaders would put her in jail too, because she had helped Paul and Silas. Even though she was afraid, Lydia was still glad that she had invited them stay at her house.

Soon Lydia's whole family was baptized. Then Prisca and her other friends were baptized. Lydia became a leader of a brand new church.

The Man at the Pool

BASED ON JOHN 5:1–9

One day when Jesus was in Jerusalem, he went to a place called Bethzatha. There was a pool full of water there. And there were many people gathered around the pool. They were all sick. Some couldn't walk. Some of them couldn't see and some couldn't hear.

Jesus went up to a man who was lying on a mat near the edge of the pool. "Why are all these sick people gathered around this pool?"

The man looked up a Jesus. "Don't you know? We are all waiting for the water to start moving. That mean's an angel is stirring the water."

"Then what happens?" Jesus asked.

"Well, the first one into the water after the angel stirs it up – the first one to get in – is healed. Whatever is wrong with them is made better."

"Have you been here when the water is stirred up?"

"Yes, but I can never get into the water fast enough."

"Why not?"

"Because I can't walk or run. And I don't have any family or friends to help me into the pool."

"Do you want to be strong again? Do you want to be able to walk?" Jesus asked.

"Of course," said the man. "But somebody always gets into the pool before I do."

"Stand up and walk," said Jesus.

"What?" The man looked very puzzled.

"Stand up and walk."

So the man tried to get up. He felt shaky. But he was able to stand. And then he took a step. And another one. And another one.

"Look!" he yelled. "I can walk! I can walk!"

SEVENTH SUNDAY OF EASTER

A Nine-Year-Old Slave

BASED ON ACTS 16:16–24

Note to parents and leaders: *Ascension Day happens at this point in the liturgical year. Those who wish to use Ascension Day readings instead of the readings for the Seventh Sunday of Easter can find a story based on the Ascension Day readings in the* Lectionary Story Bible, Year A, *page 114.*

Important note: This is not a happy story. Paul removes the problem of Claudia's "gift" for his own selfish reasons. As a result, Claudia is left in a worse situation than before. But that's the way real life is. Please help the children understand that not all stories have a happy ending.

The children may also be concerned about the matter of slavery. It may be hard for them to understand that while slavery was acceptable in biblical times, it is not what God wanted then or now.

In Bible days, most people thought it was okay to own slaves – people who had to do everything you wanted them to do. Today we don't think God wants us to have slaves. God wants us to love each other, and to be fair and kind. God doesn't want one person to own another person, the way you might own a dog or a horse.

Claudia was nine years old. She was a slave.

Claudia was very smart. Even though she was only nine years old, she could look at you and tell what was going to happen in your life. The people who owned Claudia took her to the market. They told people, "If you give us some money, our slave Claudia can tell what is going to happen." Claudia's owners were getting very rich.

One day, Paul and his friend Silas were walking through the market. When Claudia saw them, she knew right away that these men were different. "These men belong to God!" she shouted. "They are here to tell us how to live God's way."

"How did you know that?" Paul asked.

Claudia shrugged her shoulders. "I just knew, that's all."

"Well, don't say anything right now," said Paul. "When we're ready, we'll have a big meeting and we'll tell everybody about Jesus."

"Take me with you," said Claudia. "I hate it when I have to go around telling people what's going to happen. Please let me come with you."

"We can't do that," said Paul. "You are a slave and you belong to your owners."

Paul and Silas walked away, but Claudia just stood there. She had tears in her eyes. Then suddenly she ran after them. "These men belong to God!" she yelled.

Claudia followed Paul and Silas all day. And she yelled, over and over, "These men belong to God and they have come to tell us how to live God's way."

"Go back to your owners," Paul said. "I have a headache, and I'm tired, and I don't like it when you follow us."

"Yeah," said Silas. "Stop following us and yelling. Go away!"

Claudia looked down at the ground. For a while she just stood there with the two men who looked angry.

"No," she finally said. "I don't want to be in the market all the time telling people what will happen. I hate doing that."

"All right!" said Paul. Claudia could see that he was angry. "We'll get rid of that spirit in you that helps you tell people what is going to happen."

Then Paul put is hand on Claudia's head. He looked up at the sky. Then he yelled very loud. Everyone in the market looked at them. "Spirit! Come out of Claudia! Jesus doesn't want you to be in Claudia anymore!"

And Claudia knew right then that she wouldn't be able to tell people what was going to happen to them. When her owners heard Paul yelling, they came running.

"What happened?" they asked Claudia.

"Those men took the spirit out of me. I can't tell what's going to happen anymore."

"What!" her owners yelled. "They shouldn't have done that. Now we can't get money from people who want to know what's going to happen to them." So the owners got some of their friends to help them grab Paul and Silas. They tied them up and dragged them to the judge in the court.

"You did a bad thing!" said the judge. Then the judge called some helpers. "Give these men a good beating and then throw them in jail."

Late that night, Paul and Silas were sitting in the dark in the jail wondering what would to happen to them.

Outside the jail, Claudia was wondering what would happen to *her.* "Since you can't tell people what is going to happen," the owners said to Claudia, "you will have to work very hard like every other slave."

Poor Claudia had to work hard all day long, just like all the other slaves, washing floors and cleaning toilets and digging out weeds in the garden. She had to do everything her owners told her to do.

"I wish I had never seen those two men," Claudia said to herself. There were tears in her eyes.

The People Build a Tower

BASED ON GENESIS 11:1–9

People long ago used to wonder, "Why do people speak so many different languages?" Today we sometimes ask the same question. How come some people speak French, while other people speak English or Spanish, or Urdu or Cantonese? Wouldn't it be easier if everyone spoke the same language?

When the people of the Bible couldn't explain things, they sometimes told each other stories, which helped them understand.

After the flood in the time of Noah, people and animals and birds began to have babies. That's what God had told them to do. And these people and animals and birds spread out all over the world.

Some of the people found a very nice place to live. It had lots of grass for their sheep and goats. Soon more and more people came to this place and it became a city. They called the city Babylon.

One day some of the people said, "You know what we should do? We should build a really high tower. Everybody in the whole world will come to see it. It will make us famous. We will call it the Tower of Babel."

So they started making lots of bricks. They stuck the bricks together with tar, and they piled the bricks higher and higher.

"Our tower is going to reach right up to heaven," they said. "We are the best people in the whole world!"

God saw what the people were building. God didn't like it. "Soon they'll be able to do anything they want," said God.

So God changed the words that came out of their mouths. God changed their language so they couldn't understand each other.

One person said "Yes," but it sounded like "no" to someone else. Or a word that sounded like "love" to one person sounded like "hate" to another. Soon they were yelling and fighting.

The people of Babylon didn't work together anymore. They didn't understand each other.

They stopped building the tower and moved away from each other to many different places.

That is why, when people make sounds like talking, but we can't understand what they are saying, we call it "babble." Or when a baby is just learning to talk, we say the baby is babbling. It is one way we remember the story of the Tower of Babel.

The Birthday of the Church

BASED ON ACTS 2

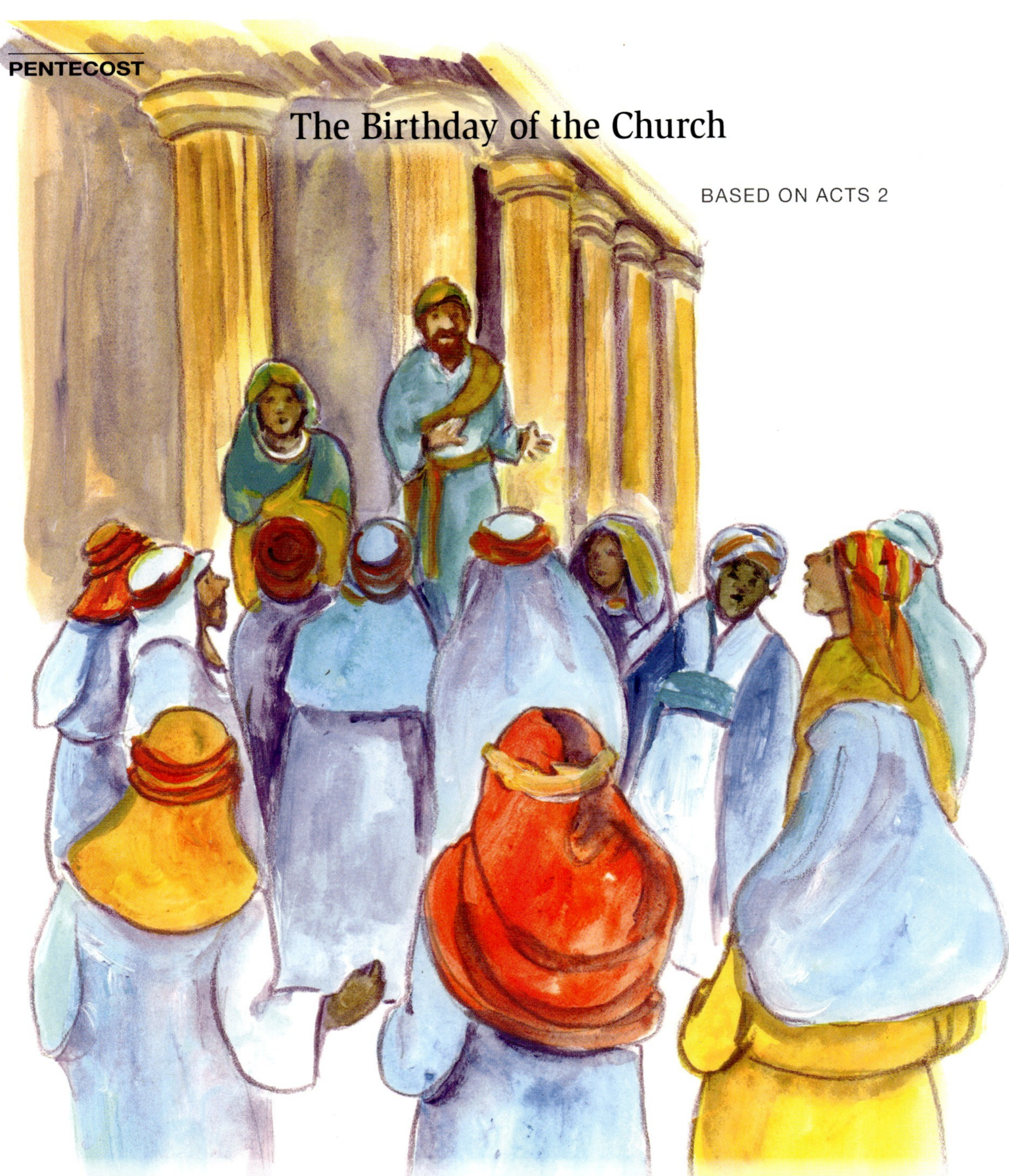

It was seven weeks since Jesus died. But the disciples knew Jesus was still alive.

One day, the disciples were all together, with many other people. It was the day of Pentecost, an important time for Jewish people.

Then something very strange happened. Some said there was the sound of a strong wind. Others said there were little bits of fire dancing around among the disciples.

The strangest part was that the disciples began to talk in new ways. Nobody was sure what kind of languages they spoke. Even the disciples weren't sure about the new words they heard themselves saying.

But others understood. "Hey!" someone said. "I come from a place where we speak a different language. How come I can understand what he's saying?"

People were there from many faraway places. They understood many different languages. Yet they could each understand what the disciples were saying.

"What is going on here?" people asked.

"You drank too much wine!" somebody said to Peter.

"No," said Peter. Then he stood up and talked to all the people who had come together for Pentecost.

"My friends," said Peter, "we're not drunk. Something very important has happened here." Then Peter told them the whole story, beginning many, many years ago with Abraham and Sarah, right up until the time of Jesus. Then Peter told them how Jesus was God's Messiah.

Peter explained that from now on, God's Spirit would be with everyone who believed in Jesus. We would not be able to see Jesus alive again the way the disciples had seen him. But Jesus would be alive in our hearts. Peter called it "the Holy Spirit."

"What should we do?" someone asked.

"Be sorry for the wrong things you have done," said Peter. "Believe that God really loves you."

Many people said, "Yes, we want to do that." So they were baptized in water. Being baptized was a way of saying, "I want to live in God's way."

The disciples were happy. Now they knew what Jesus wanted them to do. Jesus wanted the disciples to help everyone know about God's love.

So the disciples went to many places. They told people about Jesus and about God's promise.

Many people came to the disciples and said, "Yes, I believe that Jesus is God's Messiah. I want to live in God's way."

Soon there were people in many places who knew about Jesus. These people got together to help each other, to eat together, to remember the things that Jesus said, and to talk about living in God's way. When people came together like this, they called it a church.

TRINITY SUNDAY
(FIRST SUNDAY AFTER PENTECOST)

A Song from the Bible

BASED ON PSALM 8

God, you are wonderful.
When I think of your love, I feel strong.
You have made the stars in the sky
and you made me – a tiny new baby.

Oh, God, when I look up at the sky,
at the moon and the stars that you made,
I feel so small, so tiny and weak.
Do you care about children?
Do you care about grown-ups, too?

You made us, God, to be a little like you.
Because of that, we are strong and loving.
You've given us the world to take care of,
all the animals and all the birds,
and everything else in the world.

God, you are wonderful.
When I think of your love,
I feel strong.

TRINITY SUNDAY
(FIRST SUNDAY AFTER PENTECOST)

Woman Wisdom

BASED ON PROVERBS 8:1–4, 22–31

One of the books of the Bible is called "Proverbs." This book contains many good ideas about how to live God's way. We call these ideas "wisdom."

The people who wrote Proverbs thought wisdom was like a person. They called her "Woman Wisdom."

Wisdom is calling you.
She is standing where the people go, calling to them as they pass by.
"I'm calling to you," she shouts. "I'm calling everyone that lives."

"God made me at the very beginning.
When God made the world, God made me.
Before there were mountains or hills,
before there were fields and flowers,
before there was a sky,
before there was water,
before all of that,
God made me.

"So I helped God make the world.
I was God's helper.
I helped God make everything.
I helped God make people.

"God and I liked the people we made.
God and I laughed and danced
because we enjoyed
the people we made together."

A Big Argument

BASED ON 1 KINGS 18:20–39

Note to leaders and parents: *In the Bible, Elijah taunts the followers of Baal by saying, among other things, "maybe he has wandered away." This phrase was actually a euphemism for "gone to the bathroom," which is why I have used that wording here. If you feel uncomfortable using this language, you may substitute the original euphemism "wandered away."*

There was a big argument going on.

"Baal is the true God," said some of the people of Israel.

"No, that's not true," said some of the other people. "Yahweh is the real God!"

It looked as if the people who liked Baal were going to win the argument. They had lots of prophets – people who listen hard to what God is saying. But the people who loved the God we call Yahweh only had one prophet left.

His name was Elijah. And all the fighting and arguing made Elijah angry.

"Listen," Elijah said to the people of Israel. "It's time to settle this argument. If Baal is the real God, that's who you should follow. If Yahweh is the real God, that's who you should follow. But you can't have both of them. You can't worship two gods."

In those days, the people thought that the best way to worship God was to make a really big fire and burn an animal on the fire. They thought God liked the smell of meat cooking.

"Here's how we'll settle this," said Elijah. "Get two bulls and bring them here."

Then Elijah spoke to the prophets of Baal. "Make a pile of wood. A big pile. Kill one of the bulls and put it on the fire. Then pray to your god. Ask your god to light the fire for you. If Baal lights your fire, then we'll know that Baal is the real God."

"Good idea!" said the people of Israel. "That way we can find out which god is real."

So the prophets of Baal piled up the wood and put the bull on it. Then they prayed, "O Baal, come and light our fire. O Baal, answer us!" And they danced around the pile of wood, and they beat on drums and they sang songs. "O Baal, answer us!"

But nothing happened. Nothing at all.

"What's the matter?" laughed Elijah. "Is Baal asleep? Has he gone away on a trip? Maybe he's gone to the bathroom?"

The prophets of Baal kept praying and dancing and singing.

But nothing happened.

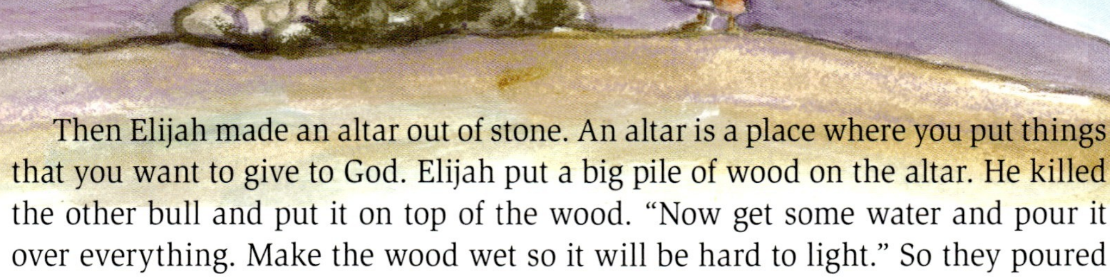

Then Elijah made an altar out of stone. An altar is a place where you put things that you want to give to God. Elijah put a big pile of wood on the altar. He killed the other bull and put it on top of the wood. "Now get some water and pour it over everything. Make the wood wet so it will be hard to light." So they poured four big jars of water on the wood.

"Do it again!" said Elijah.

So they poured four more big jars of water on the wood.

"Once more!" yelled Elijah.

Now the wood was sopping wet. It would be hard to make it burn.

Then Elijah prayed. "O God, you have always helped us when we needed you. Let all the people of Israel see, right now, that you are their God."

And just like that, the wood started to burn. It burned hard. It was very hot. The fire burned everything on the altar.

"There! Do you see that?" Elijah shouted. "Our God is the real God! Our God is the only God!"

And all the people of Israel got down on their knees and prayed. "O God, we're sorry we worshipped Baal," they said. "From now on we'll only pray to you. And we'll do all the things you tell us to do. We will try hard to live your way."

Trusting God

BASED ON LUKE 7:1–10

Note to leaders and parents: *The lectionary suggests this passage for both Proper 4 and Epiphany 9. You can find the story I wrote for Epiphany 9 on page 77.*

Jesus had been working hard all day, telling people stories about God and explaining to them how God wanted them to live. "Trust God," Jesus told them. "Believe that God loves you and cares for you."

Jesus and all the people who gathered to hear him were Jewish. All of Jesus' best friends, his disciples, were Jewish.

"We don't think you should talk to people who come from different countries," said Peter. "God loves the Jewish people best, so we think you should stay away from everybody else."

When Jesus got to Peter's house in Capernaum, there was a message for him. It was from Festus, a Roman soldier. Festus was called a "centurion," which meant that he was the commander of 100 soldiers.

"Please come to my house," said Festus. "One of my servants is very sick. I'm afraid he is going to die. Please come and make him feel better."

"Do you think I should go?" Jesus asked Peter.

"Well, yes," said Peter. "Festus has been very kind to us. He built our synagogue for us." A synagogue is like a church building where Jewish people worship God.

"Let's go!" said Jesus. He was smiling because just a few minutes earlier Peter had told Jesus not to talk to anyone who wasn't Jewish.

As Jesus and Peter were walking toward the place where Festus lived, another message came.

"Dear Jesus," said the message. "I know that some people think you shouldn't help anyone who comes from another country, and that you shouldn't talk to anyone who isn't Jewish. I know that you are not supposed to go inside the house of someone who isn't Jewish. I also know that you have the power to make good things happen. I know that all you have to do is say it, and my servant will be well again."

"Look at that," Jesus said to Peter. "I've been telling all the people around here to trust God. But here's a soldier who, even though he comes from another country, believes God can help him."

Peter laughed. "He trusts God more than most of us do!"

Then Jesus sent a message back to Festus. "Festus, I'm glad that you trust God. Your servant will get better."

The Prophet Elijah

BASED ON 1 KINGS 17:7–24

Note to leaders and parents: _This reading is also suggested for Proper 27, Year B._

After King Solomon died, there were many other kings. The worst one was King Ahab. King Ahab didn't care at all about living in God's way. He killed many of God's prophets. Jezebel, his wife, told people to worship other gods.

Then Elijah the prophet went to Ahab and said, "I have a message for you from God. Because you are worshipping other gods, there will be no rain in Israel for a long time."

That made King Ahab very angry. He wanted to kill Elijah. So Elijah ran far away into the mountains.

At first, Elijah didn't know where he would stay or how he would get food and water. But God told Elijah that a kind woman would look after him.

Then Elijah saw a woman gathering sticks of wood for her fire. "Would you get me a little drink of water?" he asked the woman. "And could I have a small piece of bread too?"

"I'm sorry," said the woman. "I don't have any bread. I'm gathering a few sticks to take home to make the last meal for my son and me. I have just a handful of flour and a little bit of cooking oil. When we have eaten that, we will starve."

"Don't be afraid," said Elijah. "Go home. First make a small piece of bread for me. Then make some bread for yourself. There will be enough flour and oil."

The woman did what Elijah said and found that she had enough flour and oil for both of them. There was even some left over. The next day, she made some more bread, and there was still flour and oil left over.

This went on day after day and the flour and the oil never ran out.

One day, the woman's son got sick. Each day, the boy got sicker and sicker, and then he stopped breathing.

"You are God's prophet," the woman cried to Elijah. "Did you come here to kill my child?"

"Give me your child," Elijah said. He took the boy in his arms and carried him upstairs to his own bed. Elijah called out to God, "Did you do this, God? This woman has been very kind to me. Why did this happen?"

Elijah held the boy very tightly in his arms and called to God over and over. "Please let this boy's life return to him." After a while, the boy began to breathe. He was alive. Elijah picked him up and carried him downstairs to his mother.

"Look," said Elijah, "Your son is alive!"

The woman was very happy. "Now I know that your God is the real God. I know that you are God's prophet."

PROPER 5

The Old Woman's Son

BASED ON LUKE 7:11–17

Jesus went to many different places to tell people about God's love. One day, as he was walking to a town called Nain, Jesus saw a large crowd of people coming out of the town. They were carrying a dead man whom they were going to bury.

Walking nearby was an old woman who was crying and shaking her head.

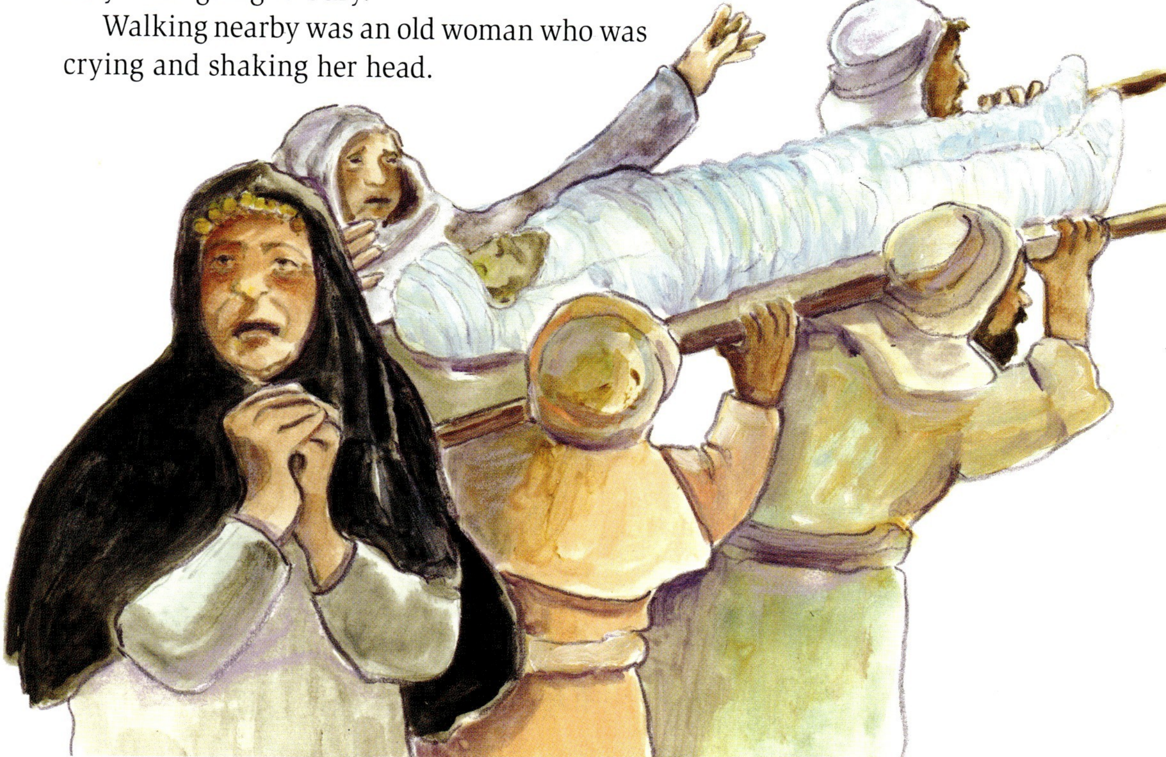

"Was this your son?" Jesus asked the woman.

She nodded. "He was my only child. My husband is dead, and now that my son is dead, I have nobody to look after me."

Jesus put his hand on the woman's shoulder. "It's going to be all right," he said. Then he walked over and touched the dead man. "Young man," said Jesus. "Get up!"

The man sat up. He rubbed his eyes. "What happened?" he asked.

The people were all very happy. Especially the old woman. "Jesus must be God's special messenger," they said. "Look what he's done! This man was dead, but now he's alive again."

PROPER 6

The Woman Who Washed Jesus' Feet

BASED ON LUKE 7:36–50

Note to leaders and parents: *One of the suggested readings for this Sunday is 2 Samuel 11:26 – 12:10, 13–15, which is the second half of the David and Bathsheba story. You can find the entire story in the* Lectionary Story Bible, Year B, *on page 163.*

In Jesus' day, people didn't have cars or airplanes or buses to travel in. If they wanted to go somewhere, they had to walk. And there was no pavement, so the roads were very dusty.

When people came to visit, their feet felt hot and dirty. It felt so good to have someone wash their feet. It was a very kind thing to do. It helped people feel welcome.

"Will you come to my house for dinner?" a man asked Jesus. The man was a Pharisee, a very important leader.

There was lots of food on the table at the Pharisee's house. Jesus could tell that he had plenty of money. He also had lots of servants. But he didn't bother to get anyone to wash Jesus' feet.

While they were eating, a woman came running into the house. Her dress was torn. She was thin. She was dirty. Many awful things had happened to her.

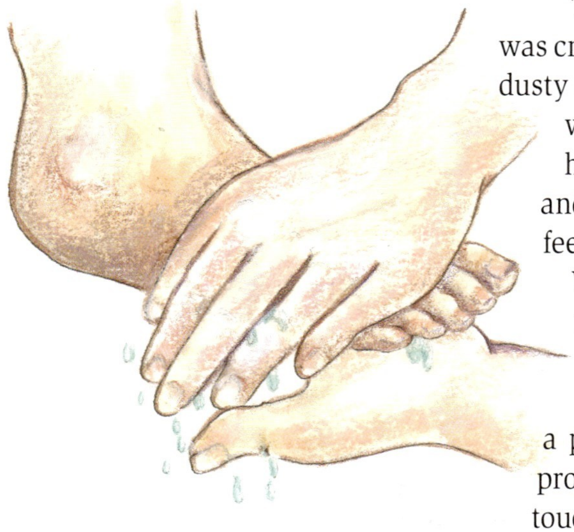

The woman came up to Jesus. She was crying. She let her tears fall on Jesus' dusty feet. Then she kissed his feet and wiped them clean and dry with her hair. She opened a jar of perfume and rubbed the perfume on Jesus' feet.

When the Pharisee saw this, he frowned. "Doesn't Jesus know who this woman is?" he thought. "Doesn't he know what kind of a person she is? If Jesus really is a prophet, he'd know she shouldn't be touching him at all."

Jesus could see the Pharisee's face. He could guess what the man was thinking.

"I have something to say to you," Jesus said.

"Of course, teacher," the Pharisee said very politely.

Then Jesus told the Pharisee a little story. A parable.

"Two people owed some money to a banker," said Jesus. "One person owed 200 dollars. The other person owed only two dollars. Neither person had any money to pay the banker. So the banker said to each of them, 'You don't have to pay the money back.'

"Now," asked Jesus, "which one will love the banker more?"

"The one who owed the most," said the Pharisee.

"That's right," said Jesus. "When I came into your house, you didn't wash my feet. But this woman has washed my feet with her tears. You didn't welcome me and anoint my head with oil. But this woman has rubbed my feet with beautiful smelling perfume. She has been kind and welcoming.

"Life has been hard for this woman," said Jesus. "So God will reach out to her. She feels God's love more than you do. Those who need more love will be given more love."

PROPER 7

God Speaks in a Whisper

1 KINGS 19:1–15a

King Ahab was still trying to kill God's prophets. Jezebel, King Ahab's wife, sent some of her servants to find Elijah and kill him. Elijah was afraid.

"Oh, God," said Elijah. "Everything is going wrong. The people of Israel are turning away from you. They are helping King Ahab and Jezebel kill your prophets. I am the only prophet left. Why don't you just kill me too?"

So God said to Elijah, "Go up to the top of the mountain, and I will speak to you there."

So Elijah went up the mountain. He listened for God's voice.

Elijah heard a strong wind that even blew the rocks around.

But the voice of God was not in the wind.

Elijah felt a mighty earthquake.

But the voice of God was not in the earthquake.

Elijah heard the crackling of a huge fire.

But the voice of God was not in the fire.

Then Elijah heard a soft, quiet whisper.

God spoke to Elijah in that soft and gentle whisper.

And when Elijah heard God's voice, he felt strong enough to keep on being a prophet.

PROPER 7

The Man Who Was Full of Bad Spirits

BASED ON LUKE 8:26–39

One day Jesus and his friends got into a boat. Jesus wanted to sail across the lake of Galilee to another country – a place called Gerasene.

When Jesus stepped out of the boat, a man came running up to him. The man was jumping up and down and screaming.

Jesus could see right away that the man was very sick. The man had no clothes on. His whole body was very dirty.

The man ran right up to Jesus and yelled at him. "Why did you come here, Jesus? You are God's child, right? Did you come here just to hurt me?"

"Tell me your name," said Jesus.

"I don't have a name!" the man screeched. "I am full of bad spirits. I am full of things that make me yell and scream and run around with no clothes."

"Would you like those bad spirits to come out of you?"

The man started turning his head in strange ways. "No, no, the spirits don't want to come out. They have no place to go."

Jesus pointed to some pigs that were on a hill nearby. "We could make the spirits go into those pigs," Jesus said.

The man didn't seem able to talk. He made strange gurgling noises.

Jesus took the sick man's hand and looked into his eyes. "Come out, you bad spirits," said Jesus. "Come out of this man. Go into those pigs over there."

Bit by bit the man stopped making gurgling noises. He stopped yelling. He stopped jumping around.

"What is your name?" Jesus asked again.

"My name is Ahaz," the man said quietly.

"And you felt as if you were full of bad things. You called them spirits. But now they are all gone."

Ahaz smiled at Jesus. "Thank you," he whispered.

"Good." Jesus smiled at Ahaz. "Let's go down to the lake and you can wash in the nice cool water. We'll find you some food and something to drink and some clothes to put on. Then you won't feel as if you are full of bad spirits anymore."

PROPER 8

So You Want to Be a Disciple?

BASED ON LUKE 9:51–62

Jesus and his friends were on a journey. They were going all the way from Galilee, where they lived, to Jerusalem. They had to walk the whole way because there were no cars or even bicycles. And they didn't have enough money to get donkeys or horses to carry them.

Many people had heard about Jesus. All along the way, people came and wanted to hear Jesus tell stories about God's love. Many of them wanted to become Jesus' special friends – his disciples.

A tall man with rich clothes came up to Jesus. "I want to become one of your friends," he said to Jesus. "I will go with you everywhere."

"Are you sure?" Jesus asked. "Foxes have cozy little dens where they sleep at night. Birds have soft nests in the trees. But I don't have any place like that. I don't even have a pillow or a blanket. I lie down on the ground at night. If you follow me, you'll have to live like that too."

The tall man looked at Jesus. He looked at his own nice clothes. "You can't expect me to sleep on the ground," said the man. "My clothes might get dirty."

"Then I don't really think you want to be my disciple," said Jesus. The man walked away slowly. Jesus could see that the man thought his clothes were more important than being a disciple.

Then a young woman came up to Jesus. "I would like to be one of your special friends, Jesus," she said. "I've heard you tell many stories about God's love. I've heard you talk about living God's way, and I want to do that too."

"That's wonderful," said Jesus. "Come with me to Jerusalem."

"Well, I can't right now," said the woman. "My mother and my father are old and they need me to take care of them."

"I understand," said Jesus. "Taking care of your mother and father is part of living God's way. You can still be my friend, even if you can't come to Jerusalem with me now."

A young man came up to Jesus as they were walking down the road. "Jesus!" he called. "I would like to come with you to Jerusalem. I've heard the stories you tell. I would like to be one of your disciples."

"That's wonderful," said Jesus. "Come with me."

"You mean, like, right now?" The young man looked very unhappy.

"What's the matter?"

"Well, ah, could I just run home and say goodbye to my friends and family?" he asked. "And I have a few things to take care of. You know – I need to be sure someone is looking after my business and..."

Jesus stopped walking and looked right at the young man. "When you make up your mind to do something, do it. You don't stop to think of all the other tasks you have to do first. If you want to be one of my disciples, come right now."

The young man looked sad, then turned and walked toward his home. Jesus took a deep, sad breath and started walking again.

Mary of Magdala was walking nearby. "It's not easy being your disciple," she said to Jesus.

"I know, Mary. People must want to be a disciple more than anything else."

PROPER 9

People Are Hungry

BASED ON LUKE 10:1–11, 16–20

Note for leaders and parents: *One of the suggested readings for this Sunday is 2 Kings 5:1–14, the story of Naaman's cure from leprosy. It is also the reading for the 6th Sunday after the Epiphany, Year B. The story may be found in the* Lectionary Story Bible, Year B, *page 63.*

"There are so many people who want to hear your stories," Mary of Magdala said to Jesus. "They want to know how God wants them to live. It's almost like being hungry for food. They want it so badly."

"But there's only one of me," said Jesus. "And when I get to Jerusalem, I may be killed. If that happens, how will they hear my stories?"

"You have us!" said Mary. "We are your disciples – your special friends. We've listened to you every day, telling stories about God's love and helping us understand how to live God's way. We could help."

So Mary and Jesus and some of the other disciples sat down together and they made a plan. Then Jesus called a big meeting. All his many friends were there. "How many people do we have here?" he asked.

Mary counted. "There are 70 people here."

"Good," said Jesus. "I want you to go to all the towns and villages around here. Don't go alone. Go two by two. Go to each of the villages, and gather the people together. Tell them the stories I told you. Tell them about God's love. Tell them how to live God's way."

Andrew had a question. "Jesus, what do we do if they don't want to hear us? What if they tell us to go away because they don't believe our stories?"

"That will happen, Andrew. Some people will tell you to go away and leave them alone. They will not want to hear about God's love. Don't argue with them. Just go on to the next town."

So the disciples went out. Two by two. In most of the towns and villages, people were glad to see them. "Yes, come!" they would say. "And you can sleep at our house and I'll give you some food to eat."

But in some places, people just said, "Get out of here." In some villages, they even threw stones at the disciples.

After the disciples had been doing this for many days, they all came together again. "Tell me what happened," said Jesus.

"It was wonderful!" said Andrew. "Well, mostly it was wonderful. Some people didn't want us, so we did what you said, Jesus. We just went to the next village. But most people really wanted to hear the stories. Most of the people wanted us to stay longer, but we had to go on to other towns and villages."

"Great!" said Jesus. "God loves everyone in this whole world, but most of them don't know it. I hope you'll keep right on telling people about God's love. They are hungry to hear it."

PROPER 10

A Big Letter to a Little Church

BASED ON COLOSSIANS 1:1–14

Note to leaders and parents: *At the end of this story, Epaphras mentions that the people of Colossae will hear more from this letter from Paul. This is a reference to the reading and story for Proper 29, on page 225. You may wish to read this story again at that time as an introduction.*

"Be sure to come to church," Epaphras said. "Something very special is going to happen."

Epaphras was the leader of a tiny church in Colossae. They didn't have a church building – they all gathered at Epaphras' house, even though it was a little crowded.

"What's going to happen?" the people asked Epaphras. He just smiled.

When everybody had come, Epaphras stood up. He cleared his throat loudly – *ahem* – so everyone would listen. Then he showed them a scroll.

"We have a letter!" he said. "Guess who it's from?" Nobody could guess. People in Bible days didn't send or get many letters. Because there were no post offices and no e-mail, people had to ask friends and other travellers to deliver their letters.

"It's from Paul!" said Epaphras.

"Wow! That's wonderful!" said some of the people. But others just looked puzzled and asked, "Who is Paul?"

"Paul has helped many, many people learn about Jesus," said Epaphras. "He has walked to many places to do that. He often writes letters to the people he has visited. He's never been here to Colossae, but he wrote us a very nice letter anyway. I will read it to you."

Epaphras unrolled the scroll and began to read.

My dear friends in Colossae,

When I talk to God in my prayers, I always say "thank you" to God for people like you. You show each other what God is like by being kind and gentle and fair and loving to each other. You treat each other the way God treats you.

You are like an apple tree. You listen to stories about Jesus. You talk to God in your prayers. And so you are

strong and beautiful, like a good apple tree. Because of that, there are lots of sweet, juicy apples growing on your branches. When you are kind to someone in your church, that's like a sweet juicy apple growing on one of your branches. When you help the people of Colossae who are not part of your church – maybe someone who is hungry or doesn't have a place to live – that's also like a nice red apple. Those apples are good food for all your friends in your small house-church.

And so I hope you will keep your faith growing. Keep talking to God in your prayers. Get together often to sing and pray together, and to tell each other stories about how you are trying to live God's way.

Epaphras rolled up the scroll. "There's a lot more in Paul's letter. He says many things about how to live. We'll read a little more of it each time we get together."

PROPER 10

The Good Samaritan

BASED ON LUKE 10:25–37

One day a lawyer came to Jesus. "Teacher," he said. "What must I do if I want to live with God after I die?"

"What does it say in the law books?" Jesus asked.

"Love God with all your heart," said the lawyer. "Love God with all your soul. Love God with all your strength. And love your neighbour the way you love yourself."

"That's right," said Jesus. "Do that and you will live with God forever."

The lawyer wanted to argue with Jesus. "But who is my neighbour?" he asked.

So Jesus told him a story about a Samaritan. In the land where Jesus lived, people didn't like Samaritans because their clothes were different and they talked differently. Here's the story Jesus told.

A man was walking down a lonely road all by himself.

Suddenly some robbers came. They grabbed the man. They beat him up. The robbers took his money and his clothes and left him lying on the road. He was bleeding badly.

First came a person who was all dressed up in nice clothes. "Oh," said the well-dressed person. "I don't want to get blood on my nice clothes. I'm going to pretend I didn't see him."

Then a very busy person came along. "Oh," said the busy person. "If I stop, I'll lose some time. I'm very busy. I'm going to pretend I didn't see him."

Then a Samaritan came along. No one expected to get help from a Samaritan. But the Samaritan looked at the man lying beside the road. "Oh," said the Samaritan. "This poor man needs help. I'll see what I can do."

The Samaritan poured medicine on the man's sores. Then he tore some of his own clothes into strips to make bandages. Then the Samaritan put the man on his own donkey and took him to an inn.

"Take care of this poor man," the Samaritan said. "Here is some money to pay for whatever he needs. I'll come back in a few days. If it costs any more to take care of him, I'll pay you."

When Jesus had finished the story he looked at the lawyer. "Now who was being a neighbour to the man who was robbed?"

"The one who was kind to him," said the lawyer.

"Well," said Jesus. "Go and be like that person."

PROPER 11

Martha Learns about Food

BASED ON LUKE 10:38–42

Note to parents and leaders: *One of the suggested readings from the Hebrew Scriptures for this Sunday is Genesis 18:1–10a, the story of Abraham and Sarah learning they will have a child. You can find that story, which really continues to verse 15, in the* Lectionary Story Bible, Year A, *on page 133.*

Martha liked to help people. She liked to work hard. She liked to help others. Most of all, Martha liked to cook. Martha could make wonderful things to eat.

Martha lived in a house with her sister Mary and her brother Lazarus. One of their special friends was Jesus. Martha liked to cook for Jesus. He loved to eat good food.

It was hard work for Jesus to help so many people. Crowds of people followed him everywhere. He talked with them and tried to show them how much God loved them. But it made Jesus very tired.

Sometimes when Jesus was tired, he would visit his friends Martha and Mary.

One day when Martha saw Jesus walking toward her house, she could tell he was tired. "You just go and sit down and relax," Martha said to Jesus. "I'll cook you some really good food."

Martha thought her sister Mary would help her. Instead, Mary sat down to talk with Jesus.

It was a hot day. Martha was working very hard. She could hear Mary and Jesus talking together in the other room. "Why should I do all this work alone?" Martha thought. "Mary is just sitting around not doing anything."

Martha was angry. She marched into the other room. "Don't you care?" she asked Jesus. "Don't you care that my sister has left me to do all the work? Tell Mary to help me!"

"Martha, Martha," Jesus said. "Don't worry so much about cooking. You are a very kind person. But you need to sit down and rest a little. Come and talk with Mary and me."

"Aren't you hungry?" asked Martha.

"Yes, I am," said Jesus. "I'm hungry for your kind of food. I'm also hungry for another kind of food that Mary and I are sharing."

"I don't understand," said Martha.

"There is another kind of food, Martha. It isn't food you eat with your mouth. It is food that helps you grow inside."

Martha wiped her hands and sat down beside Jesus.

"The kind of food you are making feeds us for a day," said Jesus. "But you and I also need God's love. It's a kind of food that feeds us for our whole lives."

"Now I see," said Martha. "We need both kinds of food to be strong."

"That's right," smiled Jesus. "So let's sit and talk for a while. We'll share one kind of food. Then, after a while, we'll both help you prepare the other kind."

PROPER 12

Sing Thanks to God

BASED ON PSALM 138

The people of Bible times liked to sing, just the way we like to sing. Many of the songs they sang are in the Bible, in a place called the Psalms. *Here is one of the happy songs they sang. We have the words, but we don't have the music. Maybe you could make up your own music to sing with these words.*

Say thanks to God with all your heart.
Sing praise to God with all your might.
Thank you, God. You spoke to me.
Your love has made me strong.

Everyone will praise you, God,
because they know your love.
Everyone will sing your song,
because they feel your care.

I sometimes get in trouble, God,
but then you come and help.
I sometimes feel so down and sad,
but then you help me smile.

Say thanks to God with all your heart.
Sing praise to God with all your might.
Thank you, God. You spoke to me.
Your love has made me strong.

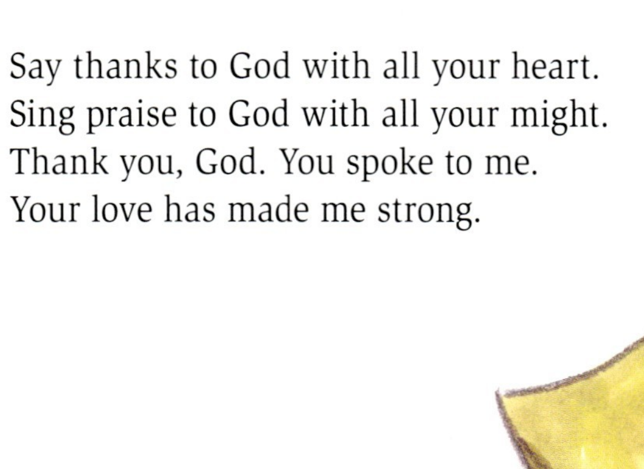

PROPER 12

Jesus Teaches Us to Pray

BASED ON LUKE 11:1–13

The prayer Jesus taught the disciples one day is sometimes called "The Lord's Prayer" or "The Our Father." You might want to ask someone to teach you the prayer the way it is said in your church. It's a good prayer to learn because sometimes when we are afraid or sad we want to pray to God, but we can't think of any words. Then we can say this prayer.

Jesus' special friends, his disciples, tried hard to grow in God's way. They noticed that Jesus often prayed to God.

The disciples wanted to pray to God too, but sometimes they didn't know what to say. One day they asked Jesus. "Please, teach us to pray."

"When you pray," said Jesus, "here are some words you can say:

Our Father in heaven,
Your name is holy.
May your peace come.
May we live on earth,
as you live in heaven.
Give us enough to eat each day.
Forgive us the bad things we have done,
as we forgive those who have done bad things to us.
Don't test us with things too hard for us,
and keep us from doing bad things
to other people and to you."

The disciples asked Jesus to say that prayer all over again so they could learn it.

"The problem is," said Mary, "that sometimes when I pray, it doesn't feel as if anything happens. I feel as if God hasn't heard my prayer."

"That's true," said Jesus. "But, Mary, suppose some friends came to your house for a visit and you were really glad to see them. And you wanted to give them something to eat but you didn't have any food in your house.

"You might go to the people who live next door and say, 'Can you lend me some food, please, so I can give my friends something to eat?'

"But the person next door says, 'No. My children are in bed and I'm in my pajamas, and you shouldn't come banging on my door so late at night.'

"So you keep knocking on the door and asking and asking until that person gives you some food just to get rid of you.'"

"Do you mean we should keep praying and praying until God is tired of hearing us?" asked Mary.

Jesus laughed. "Well, God isn't like the person next door. God wants to give you what you really need. But sometimes God says 'No.' Sometimes God wants you to be really sure that what you ask for is the best thing."

"You told us once that God is like the very best mother or father or friend that we can ever imagine," said Mary.

"That's right," said Jesus. "If you ask your friend or parent for a fish, they won't give you a stone. But if you have an upset stomach, they might say, 'No, a fish would not be good right now. Here's a glass of milk instead.'

"God listens to our prayers. And God is like the most loving friend or mother or father we can think of. Because God loves us so much, God wants to give us only those things that are good for us."

"I think I understand," said Mary. "God loves me. Because God loves me, sometimes when I ask for something, God says 'no.' Just like a good friend or father or mother. Or sometimes God gives me something else that's really better for me."

Jesus smiled. "You've got it!"

PROPER 13

When God's Children Ran Away

BASED ON HOSEA 11:1–11

Hosea was a prophet. He tried very hard to listen to God's voice. Sometimes it seemed to Hosea that he could hear God's words. Once, Hosea was sure he could hear God crying.

"My children!" God cried. "My children are running away from me. My children, whom I love so much, are running away from home.

"My children, the people of Israel, make me cry. They make me hurt all over. I am their mother. I am their father. I taught them how to walk. I snuggled them up to my face and hugged them. I fed them and took care of them.

"But sometimes they make me so angry. They go away from me and act as if nobody loves them. They fight with each other, they steal, they hate each other, they tell lies. They make me so angry sometimes.

"But what can I do? I love them so much. I get angry but I can't stay angry. I can't leave them. I have to go after them and try to show them how much I love them.

"Do you understand that, Hosea?"

"Oh, yes!" said Hosea. "Do I ever! When my wife Gomer went away from me, I was sad. Then I felt angry. But I couldn't stay angry with her. I love her. So I told her that I love her and now she and I are together again."

"And I will keep showing my love to my children," said God. "Even when they run away. I'll just keep loving them and hoping they will come back home soon."

Jesus Talks about Money

BASED ON LUKE 12:13–31

A man came to Jesus and sad, "I need you to help me. My parents gave some money to my brother and me. But my brother won't give me my share."

"Don't worry so much about money," said Jesus, "Money doesn't make you rich. You are rich when you know that God loves you."

The man shook his head. Jesus could tell he didn't understand.

"Let me tell you a story," said Jesus.

"There was a man who only wanted one thing. Money.

"He had a big house. He had a big farm, so he grew plenty of grain. He kept storing away more and more money. He didn't think about friends. He didn't think about poor people. He didn't think about God. He just thought about his money.

"Then one day the man said to himself, 'Finally, I've got enough money. Now I'm going to eat, drink, and have fun. I have enough money to last for the rest of my life.'

"But that very night the man died. He died before he could enjoy his money. He was so busy getting rich he never thought about God or about how to live. He never got to enjoy life."

A little later, Jesus was talking to his disciples about this story. Jesus wanted them to understand that it was okay to have money. But they shouldn't worry about it. Other things are far more important.

"Don't worry about what you are going to eat, or drink," Jesus said to his disciples. "Don't worry about where you are going to live. God knows that you need these things.

"Think about the birds and the flowers. They don't have houses to live in. They don't have any money. But God still loves them and takes care of them.

"Don't be afraid, my friends. Give your money away to help poor people. Try to think more about living in God's way. Living in God's way is like having a rich treasure in your heart."

PROPER 14

How Isaiah Became a Prophet

BASED ON ISAIAH 6:1–8

Note to leaders and parents: *The book of Isaiah figures prominently in the lectionary readings of the next while. This story is based on Isaiah 6:1–8, which isn't in the lectionary, but which may be useful in setting the stage for the Isaiah passages that appear in the following weeks.*

Isaiah was in the Temple that King Solomon had built. Isaiah went there to pray to God. While he was in the Temple, something wonderful happened. This is how Isaiah told the story in the Bible.

I had my eyes closed while I was praying to God. But even with my eyes closed I could see something happening.

I could see God sitting on a big chair – a throne – with angels all around. I could even hear what the angels were saying.

"God is wonderful," said the angels. "Everything in the whole world shows us God's beauty."

Then I remembered that I hadn't always lived in God's way. Sometimes I said things that weren't true.

"What is going to happen to me?" I cried. "I have said things I shouldn't have said. So have my friends and family. Oh God, what are you going to do to me?"

With my eyes still closed, I could see one of the angels take a red-hot coal. The angel came and touched it to my lips. The coal was very, very hot, but it didn't hurt. And my lips weren't burned.

"See? This hot coal has made your lips clean and fresh. God knows you are sorry for what you have done."

Then I heard God's voice. "I need someone who will talk about me to all my people," said God. "Who can I send?"

All of a sudden I heard my own lips saying, "Here I am. Send me."

When I opened my eyes, I was still in the Temple. There were other people there too, but they acted as if they hadn't seen or heard anything.

I knew then that God wanted me to be a prophet. God wants everyone to hear and understand.

PROPER 14

What Does God Want?

BASED ON ISAIAH 1:1, 10–20

Isaiah was a prophet.

A prophet is a person who looks at things that are happening. A prophet looks to see if people are living God's way, or if they are doing things they should not be doing. Then the prophet tells them what will happen, if they keep on doing it.

There are many kinds of prophets. Often, ministers in churches are prophets. Sometimes people who write in newspapers are prophets. Sometimes children are prophets, when they notice things that grown-ups don't see.

Isaiah was a prophet in Bible times. He heard people singing loud songs and he heard them saying long prayers. "This will make God happy," said the people.

Isaiah saw them burning sweet-smelling stuff called incense. "We hope God likes the smell," they said. Sometimes they roasted meat thinking, "God will like the smell of meat cooking."

"I wonder if God really likes it when people do that?" Isaiah thought to himself. So he talked to God about it. "What do you want us to do?" he asked God.

Then Isaiah went to the marketplace. He stood up on some steps and talked to all the people who were gathered there.

"This is what God is telling us," said Isaiah. "'You sing loud songs. You pray long prayers. You burn incense. But none of that pleases me.'"

"Then what should we do?" asked the people.

"God has told you what it means to live God's way," said Isaiah. "Do good things to other people. Make sure everyone is treated fairly. If someone is being bullied, help them so that the bullying stops. If there are people who don't have enough food or clothes – or people who don't have a decent place to live – help them."

"But we want to do nice things for God," said the people.

"That's how!" said Isaiah. "That's how you do nice things for God. When you are good and kind and fair to other people, you are being good and kind and fair to God."

How to Make the Grapes Grow

BASED ON ISAIAH 5:1–7

Rebekah felt sad. She walked slowly along the path to Old Isaiah's house. When she saw her old friend sitting in his favourite place under a tree, she waved to him.

Old Isaiah waved back. He was friends with all the children in the village, but Rebekah was a special friend. She came to visit him almost every day.

"Why are you looking sad, Rebekah?" Old Isaiah asked.

"I'm sad about my mom and dad," Rebekah said. "They've been working all summer trying to make the grapes grow. And now they're picking them. But the grapes aren't sweet and juicy. They're small and sour, and there aren't many of them. Mom and Dad were both so tired last night. Mom had sore knees and Dad had a sore back. They talked about pulling all the grapevines out."

"My goodness!" said Old Isaiah. "Are they going to plant something else instead?"

"I think so."

"Do you know what?"

"They talked about vegetables. Or maybe figs," said Rebekah.

"When the ground doesn't grow good grapes, that's the best thing to do," said Old Isaiah.

"But I feel sad about it."

"Of course you do." Old Isaiah took Rebekah's hand and held it against his hairy cheek. "I have a song about that in my book, Rebekah. Would you like to hear it?"

"Is it a happy song?" she asked.

"No, it isn't. It's about God's people who are like your mom and dad's grapevines. If they don't have sweet grapes on them, they'll all be pulled out."

"Well," said Rebekah. "I always like your songs, even if they are unhappy."

The old man got up slowly, and walked into his little house. He had his hand on his back where it hurt. Soon he came out with a big scroll.

"Here's my song, Rebekah. I wrote it as if God is singing the song."

Let me sing you a song,
a song about vines,
a song of sweet grapes and sour.
My love had a vineyard,
on a very nice hill,

and he dug it and moved all the stones.
He planted good grapes,
sweet juicy red grapes.
But all of these grapes turned out sour.
What more can I do?
If my vines don't grow grapes,
or only grow grapes, small and sour;
if those vines don't grow grapes
that are full of sweet juice,
I'll rip them all out. Yes I will.
If the vines are no good,
I'll plant something else.
Something else that is tasty and good.

Rebekah didn't say anything for a while after she heard Old Isaiah's song. That was okay. Rebekah and her old friend would often sit together without saying anything.

Finally Rebekah looked up at Old Isaiah. "Your song really isn't about grapes, is it?" she asked.

"You're right, Rebekah." Old Isaiah shook his head slowly. "It's too bad, but you are right."

"It's a song about God's people, isn't it? Us. If we don't live good lives – if we don't help other people and we aren't fair and kind – then we are like grapevines that don't grow good grapes. Then maybe God will choose someone else. Maybe we can't be God's people anymore." Rebekah looked very worried. She was afraid.

"No, Rebekah. That won't happen." Isaiah took her hand and held it to his cheek. "God loves us too much. But sometimes I think God feels just like you and your mom and dad feel when they work hard, but all they get are small, sour grapes."

PROPER 16

The Bent-Over Woman

BASED ON LUKE 13:10–13

Note to leaders and parents: *The story of the call of Jeremiah (Jeremiah 1:4–10), which is one of the lectionary readings for today, was also a reading for the fourth Sunday after the Epiphany.* *You will find this story on page 55.*

The Bible only tells us a very small bit of the story of the bent-over woman. The Bible doesn't tell us why she was bent over or what Jesus said to her. So I tried to imagine more of what happened and I wrote this story.

One day, Jesus was teaching in the synagogue. A synagogue is like a church. It's a place where people come to pray and to learn about God.

Jesus saw a woman sitting in the corner all by herself. "Why is she so bent over?" Jesus wondered. "Why doesn't she sit with the other people?

"Maybe people have been mean to her all her life," Jesus wondered. "I think someone has been beating her."

So Jesus called to her. "Would you come over here, please? I have something special to tell you."

Then Jesus spoke to her very quietly so the other people couldn't hear. "I think someone has been very cruel to you," he said. "That makes you feel very bad. You feel that nobody loves you."

The woman nodded her head. It was true.

"That person shouldn't be hurting you," said Jesus.

"I thought it must be my fault," the woman replied.

"No," said Jesus. "It's not your fault. It shouldn't be happening."

Jesus was angry. "And it's okay if you feel angry about it. Or if you cry.

"I have something very, very important to tell you," said Jesus. "You are God's child, just as I am God's child. You are as important and as good as anyone else. God loves you. I love you. You are God's child."

The woman's eyes began to sparkle a little. For the first time in a very long time, she stood up straight and tall.

PROPER 17

Who Is Important?

BASED ON LUKE 14:1, 7–14

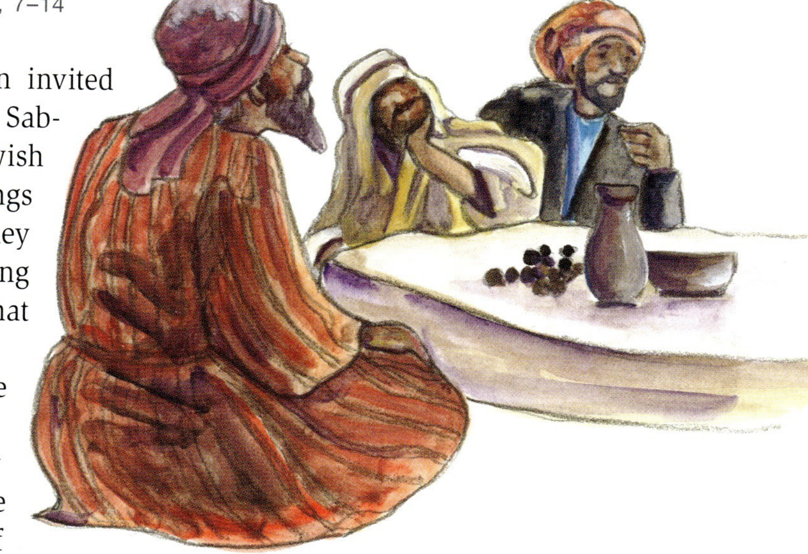

One day, Jesus had been invited out for dinner. It was the Sabbath day, the day when Jewish people stop the other things they are doing so that they can spend the day thinking about God, and about what God has done for them.

When Jesus got to the house he noticed that a lot of people were already there. Many of them were trying to sit at one end of the long table, the place where all the important people sat.

Jesus didn't like that. "My friends," he said, "when you are invited to a big dinner and there are going to be many people, don't run to try to get the most important places.

"Do you know what will happen? Someone who is more important than you may come, and then you will have to move. All the way to the other end of the table. And that would be really embarrassing, wouldn't it?"

All the people nodded.

"So this is what you should do. When you come in, go to the end of the table where all the *unimportant* people are sitting. Then someone might come and say, 'You are important. Come to the other end of the table.'"

Then Jesus sat down at the end of the table with the people who were not important. And he whispered to them. "Anyway, people at this end of the table have way more fun, don't they?"

Suddenly, Jesus stood up again. "Wait!" he said. "There was something else I wanted to tell you.

"If you are going to do a favour for someone, like inviting them for dinner, don't do it to someone who has lots of money and a nice big house. Don't invite your friends or your family or people like that. They can invite you back. And then you have to invite them back. And you just go back and forth.

"Here's a better idea. Invite someone who can't invite you back. Invite somebody who is poor and who doesn't have nice clothes or a nice house. Because when you do that, God will bless you. You will make God smile."

Then Jesus sat down again with the unimportant people at the end of the table. The person who had invited Jesus called to him. "Jesus. Come and sit up here. You are one of the important people."

"No thanks," Jesus called back. "I'd like to stay here because I'm already sitting with important people. These people are important to God. Everyone is important to God."

PROPER 18

Jeremiah Makes a Clay Pot

BASED ON JEREMIAH 18:1–11

"This is really hard work!" Jeremiah was talking to God.

"You told me to be a prophet, and that's what I'm doing," Jeremiah said to God. "But the people don't really want to hear what you tell me to say to them.

"People say to me, 'Mind your own business, Jeremiah. We can do anything we want. We don't care what God wants us to do.'"

Jeremiah just sat there waiting for God to tell him something. Jeremiah knew that God usually doesn't say words to you. God makes ideas come into your head. And, after a while, an idea came into Jeremiah's head.

Jeremiah stood right up and walked through town to a place where people make clay pots. Jeremiah watched as a potter tried to make smooth round pots. The potter had a wheel, which turned really fast.

"Thump!" She plopped a nice blob of wet clay on the centre of the wheel. Then she used her feet to turn another wheel underneath that made the wheel on the top turn really fast. With strong hands she slowly and carefully pushed the sides of the wet clay until it was shaped into a tall jug.

But not always.

Sometimes the clay would get all bulgy and lumpy, as if it didn't want to be a jug. Then the potter mushed the clay into a lump again. She pressed and pushed the clay in her hands to take out any hard lumps. Then she plopped the clay back on the wheel and started all over again.

"Aha," said Jeremiah. "Now I see what God is like."

So Jeremiah went back to the people and said, "You are like clay in God's hands. God has tried very hard to make the Hebrew people be good people. But if you don't try to live in God's way, God will do what that potter just did."

"What's that?" asked the people.

"God will mush you back into a lump and start all over again."

The people just laughed. They didn't care what Jeremiah said. Sometimes that made Jeremiah very angry. Sometimes it made him very sad.

Then Jeremiah would talk to God about it again. Each time, as he sat quietly, listening for God, something would come into his mind.

Sometimes it wasn't an idea. Sometimes it wasn't words. Sometimes it was a feeling. Often he would feel stronger after talking to God. Then Jeremiah would say, "Thank you, God, for helping me feel strong again. And even if people don't pay attention, I'll keep on trying."

PROPER 18

The Slave Who Became a Brother

BASED ON PAUL'S LETTER TO PHILEMON

Do you know what a slave is?

A slave is a person who belongs to somebody else, the way a farmer owns a horse, or a cow, or a chicken.

Slave owners can do anything they want to their slaves. They can make them work very, very hard. They can beat them. Slave owners can even kill their slaves if they want to.

Most people don't have slaves anymore because we now know that it is wrong. God loves every person in the whole world and never wants anyone to be a slave for anyone else. And there are laws in our countries that say you are not allowed to own another person as a slave.

But there were slaves in Bible times. Many, many slaves.

In our Bible, there is a letter that was written by Paul to his friend Philemon, who lived in Colossae. Philemon owned a slave named Onesimus. Onesimus was very unhappy being a slave, so he ran away from Philemon.

Onesimus ran all the way to Rome to see his friend Paul. He knew Paul, because Paul had come on a visit one time and told Philemon, and everyone who lived at his house, about Jesus. Onesimus heard Paul say, "In God's eyes, slaves are as important as anyone else. God says there is no difference between someone who is a slave, and someone who isn't."

Paul was happy to see Onesimus. "But I'm worried," said Paul. He put an arm around Onesimus' shoulder. "My friend," he said. "You know that it is against the law for a slave to run away."

"I know," said Onesimus. "But you said that God sees no difference between someone who is a slave, and someone who isn't. So why should I be Philemon's slave?"

"Maybe you shouldn't be. But if Philemon is angry, he can send soldiers to catch you and then he might even kill you."

"What should I do?" asked Onesimus.

"Can you be very brave?" asked Paul.

"I can try."

"Well then," said Paul. "I will write a letter for you to take to Philemon. I will remind him that God doesn't want people to be slaves. God thinks everyone is important and loves all of us. Then I will ask him to be kind to you, and think of you, not as a slave, but as a brother."

"Will he do that?" asked Onesimus.

"I think so. I hope so. But if you don't go back to Philemon, you'll just have to keep running and running, and someday one of the soldiers will catch you."

"Then I will be brave," said Onesimus. "I will take the letter to Philemon."

"And I will pray to God for you," said Paul. "I will pray that you will be a brave person, and I will pray that Philemon will be a kind person who remembers what I told him about God."

The Bible doesn't tell us what happened next, so we have to imagine it.

I imagine that Philemon remembered what Paul had said about God and slaves. I think Philemon put his arm around Onesimus and said, "From now on, I will treat you like a brother, not like a slave."

PROPER 19

The Lost Sheep and the Lost Coin

BASED ON LUKE 15:1–10

"How can you be a rabbi, a teacher, if you spend time with people like that?" asked Malchus.

Malchus was one of the leaders in Jerusalem. He liked to listen to Jesus talk about God's love, but he didn't like some of the things Jesus did.

"You should stay away from street people and poor people and people who do wrong things," said Malchus. "People won't think you are an important rabbi if you are friends with people like that! Today you spent almost the whole afternoon talking to that one man who lives on the street. He says bad things and he steals from people sometimes."

"That man needed a friend," said Jesus.

"I know, but..." Malchus was really upset. "How are people going to know about God's love? You should be making speeches to big crowds."

"You can't love a crowd," said Jesus. "You have to love people, one by one. Let me tell you a story about what God is like.

"There was a shepherd. The shepherd had 100 sheep. The shepherd knew each sheep by name. 'Hi, Flop Ears,' the shepherd would say. 'Hi, Spotty! Hi, Mopsy!'

"One night when the shepherd was saying good night to the sheep, he discovered that one of them was missing. 'Where is Flop Ears?' asked the shepherd.

"Right away the shepherd left the 99 sheep safe in their pen. Out into the cold and the darkness the shepherd went. 'Flop Ears, where are you? Flop Ears, it's me! Where are you?' The shepherd called and called and called.

"Then, all of a sudden, way down in a deep crack in the rocks, the shepherd heard 'Baaaaa!' The shepherd knew right away it was Flop Ears. 'I'm coming. Don't be afraid. I'll help you,' the shepherd called.

"Flop Ears and the shepherd were so glad to see each other. The shepherd hugged Flop Ears. Flop Ears snuggled up to the shepherd. Then the shepherd took Flop Ears back to the other sheep. Everyone was happy again."

Malchus understood. “God doesn’t want anyone to be lost,” he said. “It’s hard to think that God cares about one little child.”

“Well, here’s another story,” said Jesus. “There was a woman who had ten silver coins. She kept the money safely hidden, so nobody could steal it.

“One day she noticed that there were only nine coins. One of them was missing! What do you suppose she did?”

“I know,” said Malchus. “She got her broom and she swept the whole house until she found her coin.”

“You’re right,” said Jesus. “Then I think she might ask some friends to come over for a party, saying, ‘I lost my coin but now I found it again.’”

“Is that what God is like?” asked Malchus.

“Yes,” said Jesus. “It’s hard to believe, but it’s true. God loves you. And God loves that man who lives on the street. God wants to find people who are lost just like that woman wanted to find her lost coin.”

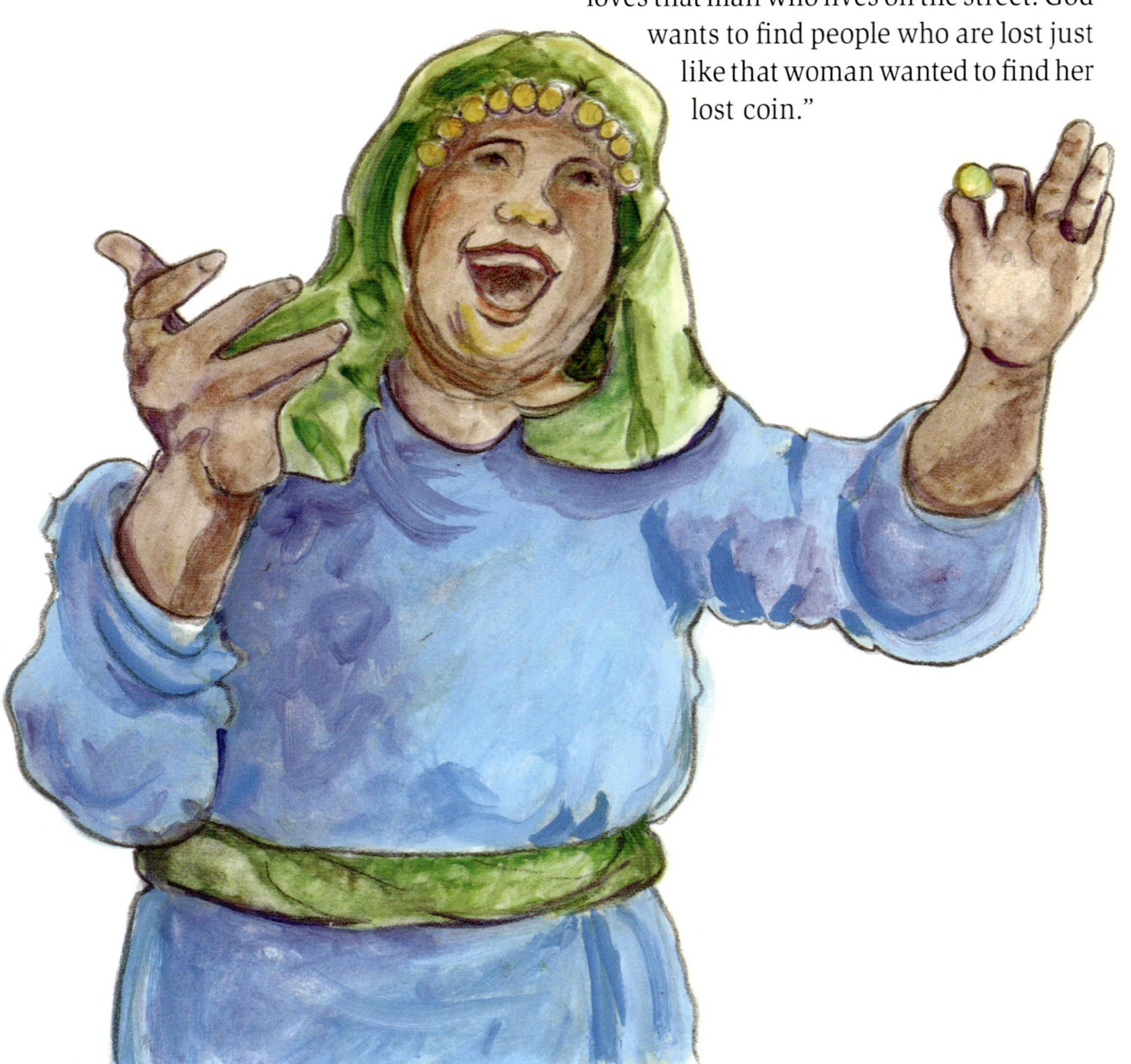

Jesus Is Joking

BASED ON LUKE 16:1–13

"I think Jesus is joking," said Mary of Magdala. "I mean he *has* to be joking. He can't be serious!"

Mary and Andrew were talking about a story Jesus told them. "I think Jesus was laughing a little when he told that story," said Andrew. "I saw his eyes sparkle as he was talking."

"Well, let's go ask him," said Mary. The two of them walked over to where Jesus was resting under a tree. "Can you tell us that story again, Jesus? The one about the man who made people tell lies."

Jesus laughed a little. "Sure. Now listen carefully."

"There was a rich man who had a helper named Simeon. The rich man saw that Simeon wasn't doing things right. Sometimes Simeon would spend the rich man's money on silly things.

"So the rich man called Simeon into his office. 'Simeon! I want you to give me a list of all the ways you have spent my money, and tell me exactly how you have taken care of all my business.

"'Yes sir!' said Simeon. But instead, he ran to the people who owed the rich man money for things they bought at his store. 'How much do you owe my boss?' Simeon asked.

"'Twenty dollars.'

"'Then look,' said Simeon. 'I've crossed it out so that it looks as if you only owe the rich man ten dollars.'

"Then Simeon went to another person who owed the rich man money. 'How much do you owe?'

"'Fifty dollars,' she said.

"'Then look,' said Simeon. 'I've crossed it out so that it looks as if you only owe the rich man 20 dollars.'

"And that's what Simeon did with all the people who owed the rich man money. They all liked Simeon and invited him over to their house for dinner.

"When the rich man heard what Simeon was doing, he said, "'Way to go, Simeon! Way to go! You're a smart man.'"

Jesus leaned over and spoke quietly to Mary and Andrew. "You see, that's how you make friends. You cheat. That's how you have to do it, if you want to be rich." Andrew could see the same sparkle in Jesus' eyes.

"You're joking, aren't you Jesus?" Andrew asked. "Because that story is upside down. The story tells us to do things we shouldn't do."

Jesus put his head back and laughed. "Of course I'm joking. But the sad part is, there are many people who think that Simeon did the right thing."

"Is it wrong to want to have money?" Mary asked.

"No," said Jesus. "But money must not become the most important thing for you. In the story, Simeon and the rich man and all the rest of the people thought that money was the most important thing. There wasn't any room in their hearts for God."

"Why not?" asked Andrew.

"Because it's like having two bosses. One boss tells you to do this, and the other boss tells you to do that. Nobody can make two bosses happy at the same time. You always love one boss more than the other. If money is your most important thing, then you can't also love God."

PROPER 21

Jeremiah Buys Some Land

BASED ON JEREMIAH 32:1–3a, 6–15

It was a sad time. It was a terrible time. The people in the city of Jerusalem were afraid.

They were afraid because there was a very big army surrounding the city. The king of Babylon had sent all his soldiers to Jerusalem. "Go and fight the people of Jerusalem. Bring them back to Babylon as my prisoners."

"No!" said the people of Jerusalem. "We will fight you!"

"That's right!" said the king of Israel to the king of Babylon. "We have soldiers, too. We'll fight you!"

"No!" said Jeremiah. Jeremiah was a prophet who helped people understand what God wanted them to do. "If you fight the soldiers from Babylon, many people will be killed. And they will win the fight because they have far more soldiers than we have. Let the soldiers from Babylon take you as prisoners. That's bad, but it's not as bad as being killed."

"Don't say that!" said the king of Israel. "We will fight the soldiers from Babylon."

"I have to say that!" said Jeremiah. "Because that's what God wants me to say."

"Then I will throw you into jail!" said the king. "I don't want you to say that kind of thing to the people in my country."

So Jeremiah sat in the jail. He talked to God about his problem. "The people are so afraid!" Jeremiah said to God. "They know that if they fight the soldiers of Babylon, many of our people will be killed. The rest of them will be taken prisoner. We will all be taken to Babylon. Soon there won't be any people of Israel left. What should I do, God? I'm in prison, so I can't talk to them. I can't tell them that you will still love them and look after them, even if the soldiers take them faraway to Babylon."

Jeremiah sat in the prison waiting for God to speak to him. After a while, he had an idea. He knew that the idea was God's way of telling him what to do.

Jeremiah sent a note to Hanamel, his cousin. "Come visit me in prison," said the note.

When Hanamel came to the prison, Jeremiah said to him, "I am going to do something strange. And I want you to tell everyone in Jerusalem about it."

"What is that?" asked Hanamel.

"You own some land outside of the city, right?" Jeremiah said.

"That's right," said Hanamel. "And all the soldiers from Babylon are walking all over it and wrecking all my plants."

"I want you to sell me that land," said Jeremiah. "I'll pay you money for it."

"But why?" Hanamel looked very puzzled. "The soldiers of Babylon have surrounded the city, and soon they will make us all go to Babylon as prisoners. You would be wasting your money!"

"That's right!" said Jeremiah. "But I want to buy that land of yours, to show the people what God is saying to me."

So Jeremiah gave Hanamel some money. Then he wrote a letter that said, "Jeremiah gave Hanamel some money, and so now Hanamel's land belongs to Jeremiah."

"Go tell everyone," said Jeremiah. "Tell everyone in Jerusalem what a strange thing I have done, and why I did it."

So Hanamel walked all over the city. He showed people the letter from Jeremiah. "Do you know why Jeremiah did this?" he asked. "Because Jeremiah wants you to know that you will come back to your homes. You will come back to your fields. You will be able to plant things in the ground once again and make them grow.

"Yes, the soldiers of Babylon will take you away as prisoners. It will be a hard time and a sad time for you. But God will be with you no matter what happens. When the soldiers take you to Babylon, God will be with you there, too.

"It will be a long time before you can come home again. But it will happen. Jeremiah will be able to plant things in the land that he bought from me. And you will come back here, too, and be able to plant things in your land.

"Jeremiah wants you to remember that God will be with you in Babylon. And God will also bring you home again."

The Rich Man Learns

BASED ON LUKE 16:19–31

Note to leaders and parents: *This story may take a bit of explaining to children if they get the idea that people who do something wrong are sent to a place of fire and brimstone.*

When Jesus wanted to teach people things, he told them stories.

The stories Jesus told are called parables. These are not stories about things that really happened. These are stories Jesus made up in his head, so that people would understand the things he wanted to tell them.

"There was once a very rich man," Jesus said, as began to tell another one of his stories. "The rich man had very nice clothes. He lived in a very big house. He always ate the best kind of food.

"Not far away was a very poor man named Lazarus. Lazarus had nothing to eat. He was sick with sores all over his body.

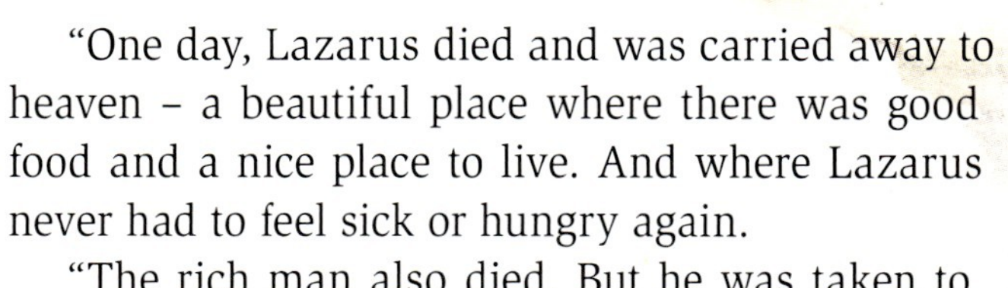

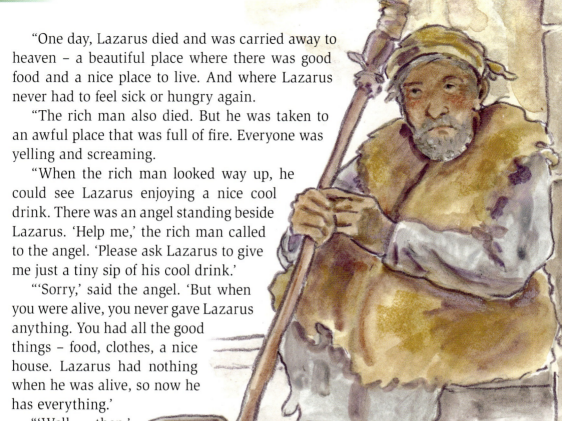

"One day, Lazarus died and was carried away to heaven – a beautiful place where there was good food and a nice place to live. And where Lazarus never had to feel sick or hungry again.

"The rich man also died. But he was taken to an awful place that was full of fire. Everyone was yelling and screaming.

"When the rich man looked way up, he could see Lazarus enjoying a nice cool drink. There was an angel standing beside Lazarus. 'Help me,' the rich man called to the angel. 'Please ask Lazarus to give me just a tiny sip of his cool drink.'

"'Sorry,' said the angel. 'But when you were alive, you never gave Lazarus anything. You had all the good things – food, clothes, a nice house. Lazarus had nothing when he was alive, so now he has everything.'

"'Well then,' said the rich man, 'would you please go to my house and tell the rest of my family what happens when they die. Tell them to be kind and helpful to those who have nothing.'

"The angel smiled. 'They have all the stories and songs in the Bible that tell them to be kind and fair to others. They should pay attention to those stories.'

"'But if an angel came to them,' said the rich man, 'they would pay attention for sure.'

"The angel smiled at the rich man, who was now very poor. 'If your family didn't pay attention to the stories in the Bible, they won't pay attention to an angel who comes to them.'"

Timothy Gets a Letter

BASED ON 2 TIMOTHY 1:1–14

Paul liked to write letters. In the Bible, we have letters that he wrote to churches in many places. Paul hoped his letters would help the people in those churches feel God's love for them, and help them to live God's way.

After Paul died, his friends kept on writing letters to each other. Sometimes they would say, "This letter sounds just like some of the things Paul said. I think I'll just leave my own name off the letter, and I'll say that Paul wrote it."

One day Timothy got a very nice letter. It began:

"This is a letter from Paul, who teaches people about Jesus. To my wonderful friend Timothy…"

Timothy knew the letter wasn't from Paul, because Paul had been dead for a long time. "Somebody else wrote this letter," said Timothy, "so that that I would remember Paul. Paul was my friend and he told me many things. We travelled to many places together to tell people about Jesus. I miss him very much."

Even though Timothy knew the letter wasn't from Paul, he read it anyway. This is what the letter said.

"I say 'thank you' to God when I think about you, Timothy. I would really like to come and see you soon.

"I know that you learned about God's love from your grandmother, Lois, and from your mother, Eunice. Now you tell others about God's love. I hope you will remember all those things you learned, so that you will always try to live God's way.

"I know it's sometimes hard to tell other people about God's love. Some people don't want to hear about it. They say, 'That's dumb!' or 'I don't want to know about what Jesus said and did!'

"When people like that make you feel bad, tell God about it in your prayers. Ask God to help you remember all the stories of Jesus that your grandmother and your mother and I have told you. When you do that, you will feel strong again.

"Thank you for being my friend,

"Paul."

PROPER 23

You Will Be Happy Again

BASED ON JEREMIAH 29:1, 4–7, 10–15

Note to parents and leaders: *One of the suggested readings for this Sunday is 2 Kings 5:1–15. It is also suggested for the sixth Sunday after the Epiphany, year B, and may be found in the* Lectionary Story Bible, Year B, *on page 63.*

The people of Israel were very sad. There had been a terrible war. The king of Babylon came with many soldiers. The soldiers fought with the people of Israel. Many people were killed. Many more were badly hurt.

"Capture the people of Israel who are still alive!" said the king of Babylon. "They are my prisoners. Bring them to Babylon so that they can work for me."

So the soldiers grabbed the people and made them walk all the way to Babylon. But they didn't take everyone. "Just bring the smartest people. The strongest people," said the king. "Leave the rest behind."

Jeremiah was one of the people left behind. Jeremiah was a prophet who helped people understand what God was saying to them. He knew that the people who had been taken to Babylon would be very unhappy.

So Jeremiah wrote them a letter. Here's what the letter said.

"God doesn't want you to sit around feeling sad. That won't do any good. Get to work. Build houses. Plant gardens and eat the food that the gardens give you. Get married and have children."

Then Jeremiah's letter said something very strange. "Don't fight the people of Babylon. That won't do any good. Help them make the city of Babylon a nice place to live. And when you pray to God, ask God to help the people of Babylon.

"And do you know why I am saying this? God made a promise. After 70 years, God will help you come back to Jerusalem. God says, 'I will bring you back to your homes.'

"So smile. Work hard. Be happy. God will bring you back home!"

PROPER 23

Jesus Heals Ten Lepers

BASED ON LUKE 17:11–19

One day, when Jesus was walking to the city of Jerusalem, he saw ten people standing beside the road.

Jesus waved and called, "Hello! Why don't you come closer and talk to me?"

"We can't. We have leprosy," they called back. "We have sore places all over our bodies. We have to stand far away so that you don't get sick with leprosy too."

Jesus smiled. He walked over to the ten people. "Don't come close!" they said.

"It's okay!" said Jesus. "It's too bad people tell you to stay away. They really don't need to do that."

Then one of the ten people looked surprised. "Aren't you Jesus? Aren't you the one who can make sick people feel better? Could you help us get better? Please!"

Then all ten of them started say, "Please help us, Jesus! Please make us better."

"Here's what I want you to do," said Jesus. "Go to a priest in the Temple – in Jerusalem. Let the priest see you. The priest will tell you that you don't have leprosy anymore."

The ten people could hardly believe this good news. They walked as fast as they could toward Jerusalem.

After a while, Jesus saw one of them coming back toward him. "Thank you," the man called to Jesus. Then when he got closer he said, "Oh, thank you Jesus. I'm strong and well again."

Jesus could tell from the kind of clothes this man was wearing, and by the way he talked, that he was a Samaritan. Samaritans came from another part of the country. They spoke a different language and they worshipped God in a different way. The people in Jerusalem didn't like them.

"That's interesting," Jesus thought to himself. "The Samaritan – the one the people around here don't like – he's the only one who came back to say thank you."

Then Jesus asked the Samaritan, "Where are the others? Weren't there ten of you?"

The man looked a little ashamed. "Yes, sir. There were."

"It's not your fault," said Jesus. "I'm glad you came back to say thank you. It's your faith in God that has made you well."

God Will Write It on Your Hearts

BASED ON JEREMIAH 31:27–34

Note to leaders and parents: *One of the suggested readings for this Sunday is Genesis 32:22–31, the story of Jacob wrestling by the Jabbok. This lection is also used for Proper 13, Year A, and may be found in the* Lectionary Story Bible, Year A, *on page 168.*

Jeremiah really wanted people to listen to what he said. That's because he was sure that God wanted him to talk about important things. But often people just wouldn't listen. They would walk away or start talking about something else.

One day, Jeremiah got so angry he went to the potter's house and got a really big clay pot. Then Jeremiah went back to the people.

"Look!" he yelled. "This is what God will do to you if you don't pay attention!"

Jeremiah threw the clay pot down on the ground. It broke into many pieces.

But the people still wouldn't listen. "Why should we listen to him," said the people. "He doesn't have anything important to say."

Jeremiah reminded the people about the promise God had made to Abraham and Sarah. "Remember the promise. Remember the covenant when God said, 'I will be your God and you will be my people.'"

"How can we remember all that?" said the people. "Prophets like you know how to read and you have time to sit with your books. But we have to work hard so that we have enough food to eat. We don't have money to buy books. And anyway, we don't know how to read."

"Listen," said Jeremiah. "God loves you very much and the time is coming when God will make a new covenant with you. It will be a covenant that you can carry inside you. You won't have to read about it in books. You won't need prophets to tell you about it. It will be as if God wrote the words on your hearts. Then you will live every day knowing how much God loves you and that you are God's people."

PROPER 24

Pray with Your Eyes Open

BASED ON LUKE 18:1–8

Jesus was teaching his friends how to live God's way. He told them this story.

There was a famous judge who wasn't very wise. "I don't care about God and I don't care about other people," said the judge. "I will do whatever I feel like doing."

One day, a woman came to the judge and said, "I sold my house to Enoch because I needed the money for food. But Enoch won't give me the money he promised."

"Go away," the judge said to the woman. "I don't want to be bothered with your problems."

But the woman wouldn't go away. She kept banging on the judge's door. "Help me get my money from Enoch!" she said. Even late at night, she would come back and knock on the judge's door. Over and over she came to the judge.

Finally the judge said, "I'm tired of this woman coming to me over and over again." So he said to one of his helpers. "Go over to Enoch and get the money that belongs to this woman. Maybe then she'll leave me alone."

Then Jesus said to his friends, "You should be a little bit like that woman when you are talking to God. Don't just pray before you go to bed, but talk to God over and over, many times a day."

"Do you mean that each time we should fold our hands and get down on our knees and say a prayer to God?" Andrew asked.

"No, no," Jesus laughed. "When you are walking somewhere, you can just say in your mind, 'Hi, God. Help me work hard today.' You don't have to close your eyes because then you'd bang into things. And you don't have to stop walking because then you'd never get anywhere.

"Or if you are playing with your friends, you can say in your mind, 'Thank you God,' for something nice that happened. You don't close your eyes and you don't stop playing the game. Or if you're walking down a busy street and you're not feeling well, you can say, 'Dear God, please help me feel better.' You don't have to close your eyes."

"For sure!" said Mary. "If you close your eyes you could bump into someone."

"Exactly," Jesus laughed. "That way you can say a hundred little prayers to God every day and nobody knows about it, except you."

"And God," said Mary. "When we pray a tiny little prayer in our minds, we know and God knows. But I don't think God is like that bad judge in your story, Jesus. God really wants to hear our prayers and really wants to help us."

"Maybe I need to make up a new story," laughed Jesus.

They Shout and Sing for Joy

BASED ON PSALM 65

The people in Bible times liked to sing. They sang when they gathered in the Temple to pray, and they sang in their homes when they sat down to eat. Sometimes, they would sing just for the fun of it.

Here are the words to two of the songs they sang.

We like to sing songs to you, O God,
because you answer our prayers.
We're happy whenever we live in your way,
and whenever we gather to pray.

You do such wonderful things, O God,
you made the mountains and hills,
you made the waves on the sea, O God,
you made the sun rise and the sun set.

You send rain to water the plants, O God,
and rivers that flow through the hills.
The plants and the grass and the trees grow green,
you did it all with your love.

We sing about all that you made, O God,
the green grass that feeds all the sheep.
Sometimes it seems that the whole world is singing,
the whole world is dancing for joy.

PROPER 25

I Want to Live in God's House

BASED ON PSALM 84

There are many good songs in the Bible. We don't know what the music was, but here are the words to one of them. We call them Psalms. Why don't you make up your own music for these words?

How lovely is your house, O God,
I want to be there with you.
I want to live with you, O God,
my heart wants to live in your home.

Even a tiny bird has a nest,
a nest for the baby
birds.
Your house would be
like a nest for me,
where I would feel
safe from harm.

A day in your house is
better, O God,
better than years
in a palace,
please take
me to live in
your heart,
O God.
Help me live
in your home
forever.

PROPER 25

Which Prayer Did God Like Best?

BASED ON LUKE 18:9–14

Jesus liked to tell stories. When he wanted to teach his friends something, he made up a story that would help them understand. Those kinds of stories are called parables.

Here's a parable that Jesus told.

There were two men who went to the Temple to pray. A temple is a very big church.

One of the men went to the Temple every week. He always wore nice clothes. He had a favourite seat near the front of the Temple. The other people who came to the Temple said, "He must be a really good man."

He prayed in a loud voice so everyone could hear. "God, you know that I am one of your best followers. I don't steal, I don't cheat, I don't tell lies. I give lots of money to the Temple. I am a very good man. You know that, God. I am one of your favourites."

The other man stood quietly at the back of the Temple. He didn't have nice clothes to wear. The people who came to the Temple usually didn't notice him.

This man said his prayer so quietly that only God could hear. And what he said was, "Dear God. I have done many bad things. I'm sorry. Please help me to be kind and fair and loving to everyone I meet."

PROPER 26

Zacchaeus Finds a New Way to See

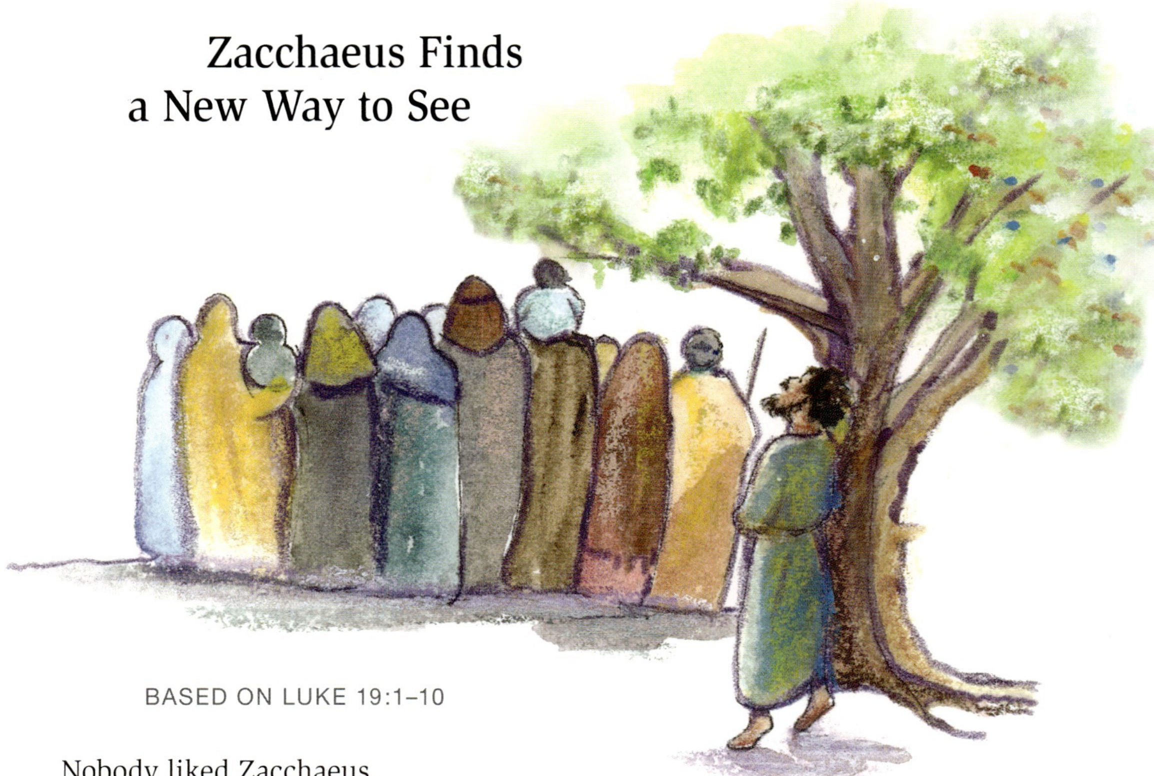

BASED ON LUKE 19:1–10

Nobody liked Zacchaeus.

Zacchaeus worked for the Romans. His job was to get tax money from the people and give it to the Roman soldiers. The soldiers took the money to the Emperor who lived in Rome.

Zacchaeus sometimes took extra money and kept it for himself. So Zacchaeus was very rich. But nobody liked Zacchaeus.

One day, Jesus came to the town where Zacchaeus lived. Excited people lined up on the side of the road. They wanted to see Jesus.

Zacchaeus knew that Jesus was a famous teacher. "I want to see Jesus, too," he said to himself.

But Zacchaeus had a problem. He was short. He couldn't see anything. When Zacchaeus stood by the side of the road, he would jump up and down but all he could see was people's backs.

Zacchaeus didn't know what to do. Then he saw a big tree near the road. "Aha!" said Zacchaeus. "I'll climb that tree. Then I can see Jesus!"

As Jesus walked into the town, he was smiling and talking to many people in the crowd. Then Jesus looked up and saw Zacchaeus in the tree. "Zacchaeus!" said Jesus. "Come down. Why don't you and I eat lunch together at your house?"

"Me?" asked Zacchaeus. He was so surprised he almost fell out of the tree. The people in the crowd were even more surprised. "Zacchaeus takes our money and gives it to the Romans," they said. "Why would Jesus want to be friends with him?"

Jesus went with Zacchaeus to his house where they had lunch together. They talked about living in God's way. Jesus helped Zacchaeus see that some of the things he was doing were wrong. "God wants you to be kind to other people," said Jesus. "God wants you to treat people the way you would like to be treated yourself."

Zacchaeus sat quietly for a long time. Then he looked up at Jesus. "Up until now, I only cared about myself. No wonder nobody likes me. I don't even like myself."

"I'm glad you feel differently," said Jesus. "Are you going to live differently?"

Again Zacchaeus thought for a long time. "Yes. I have too much money and too many things. I'm going to give half of it to poor people."

"That's good," said Jesus. "Is there anything else?"

Again, Zacchaeus thought for a long time. "Sometimes I took more money from people than I should have. So I'm going to give those people back four times as much as I took." Jesus took Zacchaeus' hand. "Something very important has happened, Zacchaeus. You've just learned how to live God's way."

PROPER 27

A Silly Question

BASED ON LUKE 20:27–38

Note to parents and leaders: *Job 19:23–27 is one of the suggested readings for this Sunday. You can find the complete story of Job, which we felt needed to be told in one piece, on page 205 of the* Lectionary Story Bible, Year B.

The Sadducees didn't like some of Jesus' stories. They didn't believe it when Jesus talked about heaven – about a place people go when they die. "When people die, they die," said the Sadducees. "That's it."

Jesus often said that when people die, their souls go to a beautiful place called heaven. The Sadducees didn't like that.

So the Sadducees tried to trick Jesus. "Let's ask him a question he can't answer. That will show people that Jesus doesn't know what he's talking about when he says there is a heaven."

"Jesus," they said, "we have an important question."

"That's good," said Jesus. "I like questions."

"Suppose a man and a woman get married. Then the man dies, so the woman gets married again. Then her new husband dies. So she gets married again, but this time she dies.

"Now all of them go to heaven. When the woman gets to heaven, whose wife will she be? Will she be the wife of her first husband, or of her second husband, because both men will be in heaven with her?"

Jesus smiled. He knew it was a trick question, but he answered it anyway.

"It's like this," said Jesus. "Things are different in heaven. Here on earth, people get married and they have children. In heaven, they don't do things like that. They are like angels, and everyone loves everyone else. So there are no husbands and wives and parents and children. They are all the same kind of people."

"That can't be," said the Sadducees. "When you die, you die. That's it. There is no such thing as heaven. That's just a silly story you made up."

"I didn't make up the story," said Jesus. "People have been talking about heaven for years and years and years."

"Oh yeah!" they said. "Name one!"

"Moses!" said Jesus. "Moses lived thousands of years ago. Moses told us that God was the God of Abraham and Sarah, of Isaac and Rebekah, of Jacob and Rachel.

"All of these people had died long before Moses said these words. God isn't a God of dead people. God loves living people who can love God back. That means all those people are alive in a new way. And if they are still alive, they must be somewhere.

"That somewhere is heaven."

God's Dream of a New World

BASED ON ISAIAH 65:17–25

It was a cloudy day. Rebekah looked up at the sky as a drop of rain fell on her forehead. She laughed a little. But then she got sad again, when she remembered where she was going. And why.

Rebekah was on her way to see her friend, Old Isaiah. She knew exactly where he would be. Old Isaiah always sat under a big tree, but if it rained really hard, he would go inside his small house. Old Isaiah had the book he was writing. Sometimes Old Isaiah would unroll the scroll and read to Rebekah. She liked to hear the words her friend had written in his book.

Rebekah didn't think that would happen today. The clouds in the sky felt like the clouds in her head. Rebekah felt sad and afraid because of what she heard her parents saying the night before. Rebekah was already in bed, but she could hear her parents talking.

"The grasshoppers have eaten all the crops in the fields," said her dad, "so there won't be much wheat this year to make bread. I'm afraid we're going to be hungry this year."

"My sister Susan told me that her family has already eaten most of their wheat," said Rebekah's mom. "I told her we'd share some of ours, but we don't have very much left either."

"All of it is made worse by the fighting," said her dad. "Our king has taken his soldiers to fight another king and his army. And they took wheat from the families to make bread for the soldiers. Why do people have to fight each other?"

It took Rebekah a long time to get to sleep. She kept thinking of the things her mom and dad had been saying. And when she woke in the morning, her head hurt. But Rebekah didn't say anything because she thought her mom had enough things to worry about.

"You don't look very happy," said Old Isaiah. He took Rebekah's hand and held it to his cheek. That was his way of saying, "I love you." Then he smiled at Rebekah and she smiled back, even though smiling is hard to do when you are worried and sad.

"Why do things have to be so awful?" she asked Old Isaiah. Then she told him everything she heard her mom and dad talking about. "People will get killed in that war. And people are going to die here in our town because there isn't enough food."

Then Rebekah and Old Isaiah sat together for a long time. They didn't say anything. Both of them were being quiet so that God could talk to them.

After a while, Rebekah spoke. "I could feel God saying things to me," said Rebekah, "but they weren't sad things. They were kind of happy."

"It's not always going to be this way, Rebekah." The old man was talking very quietly. "God says something new is going to happen."

"Could God make a better world where such sad things don't happen?" asked Rebekah.

"I don't know, Rebekah. I think God wants us to make the world a better place – a happier place."

"It could happen," said Rebekah. "It could happen if people helped each other. It could happen if we didn't have wars."

"Yes, it could." Old Isaiah was smiling now. "God keeps telling us, we can have a new heaven and a new earth. We can have a place where there is no fighting. No wars. A place where people are kind and help each other."

"Even the wild animals would be nicer," said Rebekah. "The wolf and the lamb could eat side-by-side. The lion would eat grass like a cow. Nobody would hurt or destroy things."

Then Rebekah turned to Old Isaiah. "Are those my words or are those God's words I was saying?"

Old Isaiah smiled at Rebekah so she could see his teeth, except where he didn't have any. "They are both, Rebekah. They are your words, but that is God's dream. God wants a good and beautiful world. God will help us make a world like that. But God needs our help."

"But I'm just a kid!" said Rebekah. "What can I do?"

"Think hard," said Old Isaiah.

Rebekah was quiet for a while. Then she smiled. "I have a little bag of beans I was going to use to make a necklace. Instead, I'll plant them beside our house, so when they grow we can have some beans to eat. And I know where there are some berries beside the river. I can go and get those."

"That's it!" said Old Isaiah. "If everyone does what they can, God's new world can happen."

"Are you going to write about this in your book?" asked Rebekah.

"Oh yes," said Old Isaiah. "You always help me think of good things to write about."

PROPER 29

REIGN OF CHRIST SUNDAY

Strong Inside

BASED ON COLOSSIANS 1:11–12

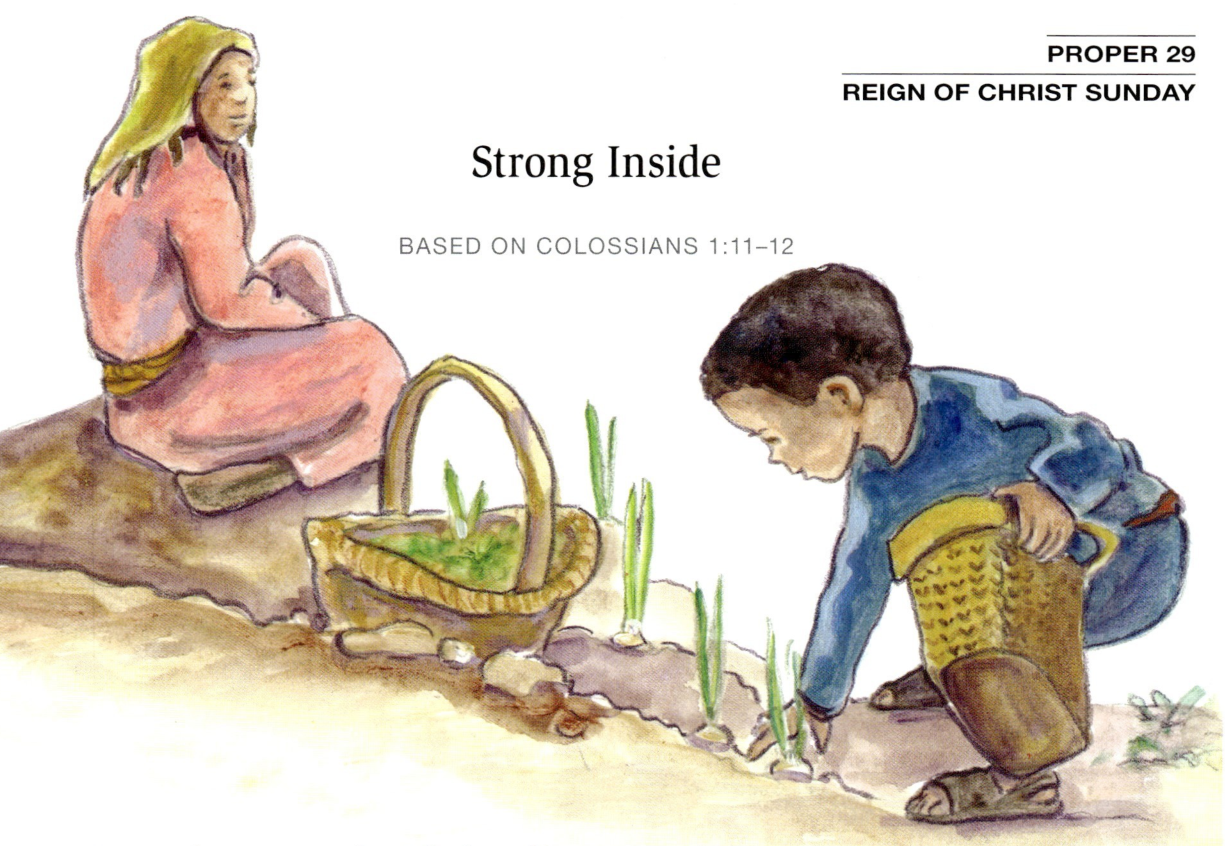

It was a hot summer day. Nimfa and her younger brother Nathanael were working in the garden. "Make sure you only pull out the weeds," said Nimfa. "Don't pull out the onions, because we want them to grow big so we can eat them."

But Nathanael kept pulling out everything. The weeds and the onions. Then Nimfa saw that his eyes looked as if he wasn't seeing anything. And his face was pale. "Are you all right?" Nimfa asked. But her brother didn't say anything.

"Come," said Nimfa. "We have to take you inside so mom can look at you." She took Nathanael's hand but he wasn't walking right. He seemed to be dizzy. Now Nimfa was really worried.

"Mom!" she called as she went through the door. "Come and see Nathanael. I think there's something wrong."

Her mother saw right away that something was very wrong. She picked Nathanael up in her arms and carried him to his bed. "Nimfa," she said. "Get a cloth and dip it in some cold water and bring it to me."

When Nimfa brought the wet cloth, she stood beside her brother's bed. "He really is sick, isn't he?" Her mom nodded.

"Should I go and get Aunt Phoebe?" Nimfa asked.

"Yes," her mom nodded. "That's a good idea. Go!"

Nimfa ran down the road to her Aunt Phoebe's house. Phoebe wasn't really Nimfa's aunt. But many children and even some grown-ups called her that, because she told them stories about Jesus and about prophets and other people who lived many years before Jesus.

Nimfa and her family were part of a small church in the city of Colossae. They gathered two or three times each week at Phoebe's house where they would sing and pray and hear the stories Phoebe told. She was the leader of this little church. And often the people in this little church would eat together, because Phoebe said that was a way of remembering Jesus – how he had been killed and came back to live with us in a new way. "Jesus is alive inside each of you," Phoebe often said when they ate together.

Phoebe was reading a letter on a scroll when Nimfa came in the door. "Aunt Phoebe, can you come to our house? My brother is sick, and my mom and I don't know what to do."

"Of course," said Phoebe. She put the scroll down on the table. The two of them walked down the street to Nimfa's house. They didn't talk. They were both thinking of Nathanael.

Nimfa's mom looked up at Phoebe when she came in the door. She took Phoebe's hand. Then Phoebe touched the boy's cheek very gently. The three of them stood there for a long time looking at Nathanael.

"Do you know what's wrong with him, Aunt Phoebe?" Nimfa asked.

"No, I don't. But I think Nathanael's going to be sick for a long time." Again, the three of them stood there. None of them really knew what to do or say.

Then Phoebe took a deep breath. "I was reading a letter when Nimfa came into my house. It was a very good letter."

"Did the letter tell you how to make my brother not be sick anymore?" asked Nimfa.

"No. And I don't know how to make him better either. But the letter said God will help you be strong, so that you and your mother can help Nathanael while he is sick. The letter I was reading said that you will find God's love inside you when you pray. That will make you strong, even when you are very tired and very worried about your brother. Nimfa, why don't you run over to my house and get that letter, so that I can read some parts of it to you."

Nimfa ran as fast as she could. When she got back, she gave the scroll to Phoebe.

"Here's what this letter tells us," Phoebe said as she unrolled the scroll.

"I will pray to God that you will be strong enough even when it takes a long time for things to happen. I'm not talking about being strong like someone with big muscles. I'm talking about being strong inside – deep, down inside so that when bad things are happening, you can even feel happy. And you will find yourself saying 'thank you' to God who helps you be strong."

Then Phoebe took Nathanael's hand for a while. She touched his cheek again. She gave Nimfa and her mom long hugs, and then went back to her house.

And Nimfa knew that she and her mom would be able to help Nathanael get well again, even if it took a long time.

Love Your Enemies

BASED ON LUKE 6:20–31

Jesus walked to many different places. He wanted to tell everyone about God's love. He wanted people to know how to live God's way.

"People don't know how to let God love them. It's almost as if they are locked inside a house. God can't get in and they can't get out."

Here are some of the things Jesus said to the people, so that they might know how to live God's way.

If you are poor,
God loves you in a special way.

If you are hungry,
God will give you a new kind of food.

If you are crying,
God will help you laugh.

Jesus also said, "It can be hard to live God's way. Sometimes people say mean things about you because you are my friend. Be glad, because God has something really wonderful in mind for you."

If you are rich,
All your money won't make you happy.

If you have lots of food,
You'll still feel hungry for God.

If everyone always says nice things about you,
you'll soon find out that they don't always mean it.

So try really hard to love people who are mean to you.
Do nice things for people who hurt you.
It's easy to be nice to your friends.

It's not hard to be kind to people who are kind to you.
But I'm asking you to do a hard thing.
I'm asking you to love your enemies.
Mostly I'm asking you to treat others just as you want to be treated yourself.

The People Say Thanks

BASED ON DEUTERONOMY 26:1–11

After the people of Israel escaped from Egypt, they lived in the desert for 40 years. They often didn't have enough food to eat or enough water to drink.

Then their leader, Moses, brought them into a new country where there was plenty to eat and drink. So they asked each other, "What should we do to say thank you to God for bringing us to this wonderful country?"

This is what they decided.

"Every year, when we gather all the food from the fields, we should remember that God gave us this food.

"We should give some of it back to God. If we have ten baskets of grain, we should give the first basket to God. If we have ten bunches of grapes, we should give the first bunch to God. If we have ten new lambs in our flock, we should give the first one to God."

"But how are we going to do that?" some of the people asked. "God is everywhere. And anyway, God doesn't need food or clothes. God isn't a person like you or me."

Then the people of Israel had a good idea. "We'll take these things to the Temple." A temple is like a big church. "Then people who are hungry can go to the Temple and get some food. And people who need clothes can go there and get something to wear.

"That way, we can always say thank you to God. Because God has given us so many good things. And when we help people who are hungry or lonely or hurt, we are doing it for God. Then we are living God's way."

Sing Out Loud!

BASED ON PSALM 100

Sometimes we are sad. Sometimes we are just... well... nothing special. And sometimes we are very happy.

People in Bible times felt the same way. Here is one of the happy songs they liked to sing. You could make up your own music to go with these words.

Be happy and dance, everyone!
Make noise and laugh and shout.
When you go to God's church
Sing out, loud and strong.
Be happy, and dance, everyone!

Be happy, because God made you.
God did it all. Not you.
We are God's people.
We are God's family.
We're happy, because God made us.

When you go into church, start singing.
When you go into church, say "Thanks!"
Say thanks to God, say it strong, and out loud.
God loves us and always has.
God loves us and always will.

Combined Scripture Index for Years A, B, and C

(Note: the letter in front of the page number denotes the volume in which the story can be found.)

Dr. RALPH MILTON is a gifted storyteller, and the author of 18 books, including the bestselling *Family Story Bible; Angels in Red Suspenders; The Spirituality of Grandparenting,* and *Julian's Cell*, a novel based on the life of Julian of Norwich. On the Internet, Ralph Milton publishes the popular e-zine Rumors, which uses liberal doses of humour and story to communicate a lively faith. Co-founder of Wood Lake Publishing, Ralph Milton lives in Kelowna, British Columbia, with his wife and friend of 50 years, Beverley, a retired church minister. Together, they remain the ever-proud grandparents of Zoë and Jake.

MARGARET KYLE has been a part of the creative process at Wood Lake Publishing for over 20 years. She has illustrated many children's books including the bestselling *Family Story Bible* by Ralph Milton (1996) and *After the Beginning* by Carolyn Pogue (2006). Margaret's artwork graces the cover of *More Voices* (2007) supplement to *Voices United* (United Church of Canada).

She lives in Okanagan Centre, British Columbia, with her husband, Michael Schwartzentruber.